The Power of Modern Value Investing

"Gary and Margaret have hit the ball out of the park with this enthralling text. From an analysis of historical bubbles and the importance of future expectations for stock values to identifying issues in measuring risk while highlighting the spurious nature of various quantitative factors, both amateur and professional investors would be well-rewarded by reading and re-reading *The Power of Modern Value Investing: Beyond Indexing, Algos, and Alpha*. I give it my highest endorsement."

—Brian Nelson, *CFA, President, Valuentum Securities*

"Gary and Margaret Smith have written a book about investing that every investor should read and keep visible on their bookshelf. They review the history of investment models and fads and find them all wanting in one way or another. They make a very convincing case for 'value investing' in stocks that return cash to investors through dividends and buybacks. Their commonsense approach leads to the conclusion that stocks and other assets that generate a cash flow for investors are the sure and steady way to accumulate wealth."

—Ed Yardeni, *President & Chief Investment Strategist, Yardeni Research, Inc.*

"According to Mark Twain, 'It ain't what you don't know that gets you in trouble. It's what you know that ain't so.' In this new book, Gary and Margaret Smith point out what ain't so with today's investing sacred cows like CAPM, mean-variance analysis, factor models, indexing, and modern portfolio theory. The Smiths make the case instead for value investing as originally conceived by John Burr Williams and Benjamin Graham. This book should be required reading for all value investors and anyone else wanting to see things differently."

—Gary Antonacci, *author of* Dual Momentum Investing

"Professors Smith provide a comprehensive review and critique of popular academically endorsed investment techniques, and describe a superior 'value oriented' analytical approach to investing in stocks."

—Chris Dialynas, *Managing Director, PIMCO*

"The Smiths debunk the common misperceptions of most investors and lay out the evolution of *Modern Value Investing*. An enjoyable read and a great road map for building wealth!"
—Andrew D. Sloves, *Board of Directors, Rithm Capital; Former Managing Director, J.P. Morgan*

"*The Power of Modern Value Investing* is the path to prosperity and an essential read for every investor. Professors Gary and Margaret Smith expertly guide readers towards enhancing their personal finances through the practical and intuitive principles of value investing. If you want to learn how to invest wisely and profitably, *The Power of Modern Value Investing* is for you."

—Mitch Mokhtari, *Professor of Personal Finance, University of Maryland—College Park*

"Gary and Margaret offer insights on how fundamental cash flow-based forecasting is the best approach to valuing a business. It provides a great foundation for both new and veteran investors. They cover asset classes ranging from cash to gold to real estate to private equity and cryptocurrencies. Having worked in finance for almost 30 years and invested in and acquired dozens of companies, I have never used the theoretical models to actually buy a business. I have used fundamental cash flow analysis they prescribe."

—Matt Thompson, *Private Equity and Technology Investor*

"Investors have understandably been 'bedazzled' by beautiful math intended to reclassify investing as a predictive science devoid of risk. However, despite its valuable insights into diversification, the industry should have decommissioned Modern Portfolio Theory (MPT) long ago. The Professors Smith do a wonderful job outlining the evolution of investment thought into bite-sized epochs that explain how the industry got into the current morass of chasing fads and past performance, rather than critically thinking about the prospects of its investments. A voracious consumer of investment philosophy, I have read over 40,000 pages on value investing alone, and Professors Smith and Smith continue to prescribe (and practice!) an accessible framework that not only upholds the original tenets of the discipline but one that investors can successfully apply across any epoch in economic history using modern statistical tools."

—Roberto Hamilton, *CFA*

Gary Smith · Margaret Smith

The Power of Modern Value Investing

Beyond Indexing, Algos, and Alpha

Gary Smith
Pomona College
Claremont, CA, USA

Margaret Smith
Newport Beach, CA, USA

ISBN 978-3-031-45899-6   ISBN 978-3-031-45900-9   (eBook)
https://doi.org/10.1007/978-3-031-45900-9

© The Editor(s) (if applicable) and The Author(s), under exclusive license to Springer Nature Switzerland AG 2023

This work is subject to copyright. All rights are solely and exclusively licensed by the Publisher, whether the whole or part of the material is concerned, specifically the rights of translation, reprinting, reuse of illustrations, recitation, broadcasting, reproduction on microfilms or in any other physical way, and transmission or information storage and retrieval, electronic adaptation, computer software, or by similar or dissimilar methodology now known or hereafter developed.
The use of general descriptive names, registered names, trademarks, service marks, etc. in this publication does not imply, even in the absence of a specific statement, that such names are exempt from the relevant protective laws and regulations and therefore free for general use.
The publisher, the authors, and the editors are safe to assume that the advice and information in this book are believed to be true and accurate at the date of publication. Neither the publisher nor the authors or the editors give a warranty, expressed or implied, with respect to the material contained herein or for any errors or omissions that may have been made. The publisher remains neutral with regard to jurisdictional claims in published maps and institutional affiliations.

Cover illustration: © Yuliia Duliakova

This Palgrave Macmillan imprint is published by the registered company Springer Nature Switzerland AG
The registered company address is: Gewerbestrasse 11, 6330 Cham, Switzerland

Paper in this product is recyclable.

Contents

1	Investing 1.0—Blind Faith and Speculation	1
2	Investing 2.0—The Birth of Value Investing	17
3	Investing 3.0—(Mis)measuring Risk	39
4	Investing 4.0—Efficient Markets and Value-Agnostic Indexing	67
5	Investing 5.0—Factor Models, Algorithms, and Chasing Alpha	85
6	Investing 6.0—Modern Value Investing	103
7	A Case Study—Stocks	119
8	A Case Study—Homes	133
9	The 9 Pitfalls of Investing	147
Index		177

List of Figures

Fig. 1.1	The South Sea Company Bubble (*Credit* These data are from Larry Neal)	3
Fig. 1.2	Tulip Bulb Prices, November 1636 to March 1637	7
Fig. 1.3	The Bicycle Bubble (*Credit* These data are from Michael Quinn)	9
Fig. 1.4	The RCA Pump-and-Dump	13
Fig. 1.5	The Roaring Twenties and the Great Crash	14
Fig. 2.1	Present value of $10 annual dividends	21
Fig. 2.2	Present value of dividends starting at $10 and increasing by 4% each year	23
Fig. 2.3	A $10,000 investment in Oracle or the S&P 500 after Oracle crashed in 1997	25
Fig. 2.4	A $10,000 investment in Apple or the S&P 500 after Apple crashed in 2013	25
Fig. 2.5	The S&P 500 dividend yield D/P and 10-year Treasury rate R, 1871–2023	29
Fig. 2.6	The S&P 500 price-earnings ratio, 1871–2023	30
Fig. 2.7	The S&P 500 earnings yield E/P and 10-year Treasury rate R	32
Fig. 2.8	The real 10-year Treasury rate and the cyclically adjusted earnings yield (CAEP)	33
Fig. 2.9	S&P 500 dividends and share repurchases	34
Fig. 2.10	The intrinsic value of the S&P 500 for different required rates of return	36
Fig. 3.1	A normal distribution with a 10% mean and 20% standard deviation	40

viii   List of Figures

Fig. 3.2	Two normal distributions	40
Fig. 3.3	The Markowitz Frontier	41
Fig. 3.4	Combining a safe investment with a risky investment	43
Fig. 3.5	The optimal risky portfolio	43
Fig. 3.6	S&P 500 monthly returns, 1926 through 2022	45
Fig. 3.7	Correlation between average monthly returns in 2003–2007 and 2008–2012	47
Fig. 3.8	Correlation between standard deviations of monthly returns	48
Fig. 3.9	Relationship between correlations of monthly returns	49
Fig. 3.10	Historical returns can lead to unbalanced portfolios	49
Fig. 3.11	Really, really bad timing	60
Fig. 3.12	Annual returns for best, worst, and average starting months	61
Fig. 3.13	Safe and sorry	63
Fig. 4.1	An immediate reaction in an efficient market	68
Fig. 4.2	Average cumulative excess returns after a big day	69
Fig. 4.3	The bitcoin roller coaster	75
Fig. 4.4	Comparing two hypothetical mutual funds	77
Fig. 4.5	Risk-adjusted performance of 34 mutual funds	78
Fig. 5.1	The beta coefficient gauges how a stock return is related to the overall market	87
Fig. 5.2	Apple and S&P 500 monthly returns, 2005–2009	87
Fig. 5.3	First Financial Fund five-year betas, 1991–2010	91
Fig. 5.4	Backtesting is spectacular	96
Fig. 5.5	Forecasting is awful	97
Fig. 5.6	Artificial unintelligence	100
Fig. 6.1	Modeling uncertainty about future dividends	106
Fig. 6.2	Our uncertainty about a stock's intrinsic value	107
Fig. 6.3	Our uncertainty about a stock's value surplus	108
Fig. 6.4	A 50–50 investment in two stocks with uncorrelated growth rates reduces risk	110
Fig. 6.5	A mean-standard deviation tradeoff for a portfolio's value surplus	111
Fig. 6.6	A Mean-probability tradeoff for a portfolio's value surplus	112
Fig. 6.7	Target, age, and 60/40 strategies	114
Fig. 6.8	Prevent-defense investment strategies usually lose the race	117
Fig. 6.9	An all-stocks strategy has trounced prevent-defense strategies	117
Fig. 7.1	JPM's stock price and two moving averages	121
Fig. 7.2	The WRDS efficient frontier	122
Fig. 7.3	Apple's beta coefficient	124
Fig. 7.4	JPM's beta coefficient	124
Fig. 7.5	Apple's share repurchases are much larger than its dividends	125
Fig. 7.6	Apple's shareholder income, 2013–2023	126
Fig. 7.7	JPM's shareholder income, 2013–2023	127
Fig. 7.8	Uncertainty about the intrinsic value of Apple	128

Fig. 7.9	Uncertainty about the intrinsic value of JPM	129
Fig. 7.10	The value-surplus mean-standard deviation frontier for Apple and JPM	130
Fig. 7.11	The mean-probability frontier for Apple and JPM	131
Fig. 8.1	The U.S. home price index (HPI) and consumer price index (CPI)	134
Fig. 8.2	A stock market bubble?	134
Fig. 8.3	Using intrinsic value estimates to assess the stock market	136
Fig. 8.4	Indianapolis and San Mateo home prices since 2005	140
Fig. 8.5	Inflation-adjusted HPI for 70 Chinese cities, 2005–2019	141
Fig. 8.6	Inflation-adjusted HPI for 70 Chinese cities, 2005–2023	142
Fig. 8.7	The intrinsic value of an ADU	145
Fig. 9.1	Inflation-adjusted S&P 500 and 10-year average dividends	149
Fig. 9.2	Inflation-adjusted S&P 500 and 10-year average earnings	150
Fig. 9.3	Daily prices of four prominent stocks in 2019	150
Fig. 9.4	SoftBank disappoints	152
Fig. 9.5	An upward channel	155
Fig. 9.6	A head-and-shoulders support level	156
Fig. 9.7	Clumsily staggering in and out of the market	158
Fig. 9.8	Passive income soon exceeds working income and spending	160
Fig. 9.9	Lemonade turning into a Lemon	167
Fig. 9.10	Money predicts inflation almost perfectly	173

List of Tables

Table 3.1	Some Portfolios on the Markowitz Frontier	42
Table 3.2	Mean monthly returns, 2003–2007 and 2008–2012	47
Table 3.3	The changes that Swensen wrought, percent of Yale endowment	51
Table 3.4	Inflation-adjusted means, percent	52
Table 3.5	The 2021 Yale Portfolio, percent of Yale endowment	54
Table 3.6	Wealth for buy-and-hold vs. portfolio turnover	57
Table 3.7	Frequency with which wealth violated historical minimums or maximums, percent	62
Table 6.1	Assumed stock parameters used in Fig. 6.5	111
Table 8.1	The first-year, after-tax home dividend for a home in Fishers, Indiana	138
Table 8.2	Chinese housing data	141
Table 8.3	The first-year home dividend for an ADU	144
Table 9.1	Frequency of more wealth with 100% stocks, percent	161

Preface

The images in books and movies of gold, silver, and jewelry tucked under floorboards, squeezed inside walls, sewn into clothing, stuffed inside furniture, buried in the ground, or hidden in caves are powerful. The idea that gold, silver, and precious jewels are treasures that we covet is deeply ingrained.

During the sixteenth, seventeenth, and eighteenth centuries, mercantilism dominated economic thinking in Europe. Mercantilists believed that a nation's wealth was measured by the gold and silver it accumulated. They consequently saw international trade as a zero-sum game. When the French sent gold or silver to England to pay for coal, mercantilists believed that England became richer and France became equally poorer. Never mind that France had coal to heat its homes and fuel its factories, while England had gold and silver that couldn't be used for much of anything.

In his treatise, *The Wealth of Nations*, Adam Smith argued that voluntary trade—within nations or between nations—is not a zero-sum game. If Jack uses gold to buy a cow from Jill and Jill uses that gold to buy a horse from Jack, they are presumably both better off. In the same way, if France uses gold to buy English coal and England uses that gold to buy French wine, both countries are better off. The gains are particularly large when countries do what they do best. If England's comparative advantage is mining coal and France's comparative advantage is making wine, then they should do that. Both countries will better be off than if the English drank English wine and the French were starved for coal.

In addition to making a compelling argument for specialization and international trade, Adam Smith argued that the true wealth of nations should be gauged by the productivity of its citizens. A nation's production of goods and services—either for domestic consumption or for beneficial trade—is what supports its citizens' standard of living. Stockpiling unproductive gold and silver benefits no one.

Same as it ever was, same as it ever was. Even today, many people believe that their wealth is measured by the amount of cash, precious metals, jewelry, and other physical objects they own. However, true wealth is better measured by their own productivity and by the productivity of their assets because this is what supports their lifestyle.

An important part of a person's wealth is what economists call *human capital*—the ability to earn income from a job. For those who own businesses, the value of the business is the income it generates. For those who own the homes they live in, the value of the home is the rent they would otherwise have to pay. In each case, it is not the size of the orchard but its fruitfulness that matters.

What about stocks? Too often, people tell us that stocks aren't real wealth because stock prices fluctuate day to day, even minute to minute, second to second. They never know what their stocks are worth. The reality is the opposite. The true measure of the value of stocks is not their ever-changing market prices but the income they generate—the productivity of the orchard. As counterintuitive as it may seem, stocks are real wealth, while precious metals and jewelry are essentially worthless because they produce no income.

The historical appeal of gold is a particularly stubborn illusion. In 2012 Warren Buffett estimated that the total amount of mined gold in the world was about 170,000 metric tons which, melded together, would make a cube that was about 68 feet on each side and would easily fit inside a 90-foot-by-90-foot baseball diamond. At the market price at that time ($1750 per ounce), this golden cube would be worth $9.6 trillion. Alternatively, with $9.6 trillion, one could buy all U.S. cropland (400 million acres generating $200 billion in annual income), 16 Exxon Mobils (each earning more than $40 billion annually), and still have $1 trillion left over (enough to buy two Apple computer companies in 2012). You could not, of course, literally buy 16 Exxons and 2 Apples; Buffett's point was that you could invest in a LOT of very profitable cropland and companies.

How would these two alternative investments fare over time? Buffett wryly observed that,

> *A century from now the 400 million acres of farmland will have produced staggering amounts of corn, wheat, cotton, and other crops—and will continue to produce that valuable bounty, whatever the currency may be. Exxon Mobil will probably have delivered trillions of dollars in dividends to its owners and will also hold assets worth many more trillions (and, remember, you get 16 Exxons). The 170,000 tons of gold will be unchanged in size and still incapable of producing anything.*
>
> *You can fondle the cube, but it will not respond.*

Alas, the allure of gold is hard to shake. One blogger responded to Buffett's argument:

> *The true value of the gold for the investor that chooses to buy it instead, is that in the future he will be able to exchange it for whatever he wants then at (hopefully) close to the same exchange rate he bought it for. He believes its value won't decay with time, or at least that there is less risk with it than with his other options.*

Spoken like a true mercantilist!

We have been investing; teaching investing; writing about investing; and advising investors for decades. We've learned the importance of attitudes and emotions. Too many people are bewitched by the mercantilist idea that wealth is measured by shiny possessions—the size of their house, the number of cars they own, and the cost of the watch or bracelet on their wrist. Too many think that cash, gold, and jewelry are smart investments because they can hold these in their hands and because they won't be distressed by news stories about stock market crashes.

Too many think that stocks are excessively risky. Even experienced investors, investment advisors, and portfolio managers are beguiled by mathematically sophisticated models that measure risk by the size of short-term price fluctuations. We used to admire those models, too.

Now, we know there is a better way.

We have been married for more than 20 years and our net worth has grown more than 12-fold—not by hoarding cash, gold, and jewelry—but by investing in stocks and other assets that produce substantial income. We are *value investors* and we wrote this book to help others understand the power and wisdom of modern value investing. Spoiler alert: it's not mercantilist madness.

Claremont, USA	Gary Smith
Newport Beach, USA	Margaret Smith

Introduction

There have been five distinct investment "phases" that have developed and evolved over time—a historical progression from what we call Investing 1.0 to 2.0, 3.0, 4.0, and 5.0. Some have been genuine advances that can help us think more clearly about investing. Others have been superficially appealing but actually detrimental to investors' wealth.

Many people, for example, are attracted to the hopeful idea that they can get rich by making spectacularly well-timed investments—buying gold, bitcoin, or a stock right before the price soars and then selling at the peak. This is what we call the Investing 1.0 strategy.

Margaret's father was born in Taiwan and remembers when Taiwan's stock market soared in the 1980s, luring in people who thought they could get rich buying Taiwanese stocks. What could go wrong? Plenty. Figure 1 shows the year-end values of the Taiwan Stock Exchange Index. The volatility was even greater for individual stocks and for daily prices. Margaret's father still tells stories of family members and friends who were gripped by speculative fever, borrowed money to buy stocks, and ended up impoverished. It turned out that buying low and selling high is really, really difficult. Many who tried ended up doing the opposite.

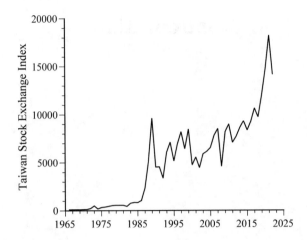

Fig. 1 The Taiwan Roller Coaster

Investing 1.0 was based on speculative fever, nothing more. Speculation is what fuels bubbles—not only in Taiwanese stocks but in collectibles, cryptocurrencies, and more. Investing 2.0 repudiated this speculative mindset and argued that investments should be judged not by wishful thinking about future prices, but by the income that investments generate. This was the birth of value investing! However, Investing 2.0 paid little attention to risk and this neglect led to Investing 3.0, which gauges the riskiness of an investment by the volatility of its market price. Investing 4.0 added the presumption that market prices are the best available measure of an investment's value. There is consequently no point in trying to beat the market—just buy at whatever price the market says is the right price. Investment 5.0 provided a more nuanced approach to assessing why some market prices are more volatile than others but it is used by zealous investors trying to predict ups and downs in market prices—a mathematically dense, computer-intensive return to Investing 1.0!

Our approach, what we call Investing 6.0, returns to the value-investing insights of Investing 2.0 but argues that risk should not be measured by the volatility of market prices.

Name Your Favorite Investment

Before we look closely at these various investment approaches, let's briefly consider the investments that people find most appealing. An April 2023 Gallup survey asked adult Americans, "Which of the following do you think is the best long-term investment?" The results:

38%	real estate
25%	gold
15%	stocks/mutual funds
9%	savings accounts/CDs
7%	bonds
4%	cryptocurrency

We agree that real estate should be one of the top picks. Houses and apartments allow people to save money that they would otherwise spend renting a place to live. Investors can also earn income by buying real estate and renting to others. Of course, all real estate is local and, like any investment, we need to consider the price. Paying millions of dollars for a shack in Death Valley is probably not a good investment. We will provide details for valuing real estate in Chapter 8.

It is not surprising but nonetheless dismaying that 25% chose gold. That age-old allure is hard to resist. In addition, the fact that nearly two-thirds chose real estate and gold likely reflects the fact that many people are most comfortable with physical investments that they can see and touch. The crucial distinction between real estate and gold is that real estate yields income and gold doesn't.

It is disappointing that only 15% chose stocks. The 2023 survey was not an aberration. Over the 13 years that this survey has been conducted, stocks have never been the top pick and have never garnered more than 27% of the votes—despite the fact that, historically, stocks have been, by far, the best performing investment. This widespread aversion to stocks is likely due to an obsession with short-term fluctuations in stock prices. If you have this obsession, we hope to cure you.

A total of 16% chose savings accounts, CDs, and bonds. At least, these investments pay interest but we will show you in later chapters why they are generally not nearly as good an investment as stocks. The 4% who chose cryptocurrencies are frankly delusional. Bitcoin and other cryptocurrencies have been called "digital gold" and this is not meant as a complement. Cryptocurrencies are like gold in that they generate no income whatsoever but they are also unlike gold, which at least has some industrial uses and can be used for jewelry. We will have more to say about both.

Cash and checking accounts were not offered as options in this Gallup survey but our experience has been that many people hold an inordinate amount of cash in their safes, safe deposit boxes, and checking accounts. The rationale is that, unlike other investments, the value doesn't fluctuate day to day. They know how much money they have. They overlook the reality that the value of their cash is whittled away, year after year, by inflation. One of our goals is to persuade cash-aholics that they should consider making income-producing investments.

A Benevolent Casino

The core principles discussed in this book apply to all investments but are most commonly applied to stocks, and we will do that too. We should begin by acknowledging that the stock market is viewed by many people as little more than a gambling casino where some are enriched and many are impoverished by wild swings in stock prices. One relative told us that decent people don't risk their life savings in casinos or the stock market. We have heard others say that the stock market is not only an unsavory casino but an elaborate con, with wealthy insiders scamming the innocent.

These fears are not completely unjustified. Stock prices can fluctuate wildly and are sometimes manipulated by scoundrels. On the other hand, the average bettor in a gambling casino loses money—that's how the casinos pay for their gaudy decorations and somber employees, and still have plenty of money left over for the casino owners. The stock market, on the other hand, can be characterized as a benevolent casino.

The stock market is like a casino in that stock prices go up and down seemingly at random, much like the roll of dice, the deal of cards, or the spin of a roulette wheel. The crucial difference between the stock market and gambling casinos is that the average stock market investor makes money because stocks pay dividends and stock prices increase over time along with the economy, corporate profits, and dividends. There have been days, months, and even years when stock prices have fallen but over the past one hundred years, the average annual return on stocks has been more than 10%. In Las Vegas, the odds favor the house. On Wall Street, the odds favor investors.

Market manipulation was rampant in the past and can still occur with small companies that have lightly traded stocks but the Securities and Exchange Commission (SEC) helps restrain such chicanery. More importantly, the volume of trading in the stocks of big well-established companies is so large that market manipulation is impractical.

The Importance of Financial Markets

The larger point is that people who go to gambling casinos are just paying for cheap (and, sometimes, not so cheap) thrills. The stock market is quite different. The stock market is part of the financial system that powers modern economies and enriches us all.

Think of your own situation. If you have a job, you might save some of your income now so that you can buy things later—a down payment on a house, your children's education, a comfortable retirement. A simple savings plan is to put $100 bills in a waterproof box and bury it in your backyard. Thirty years later, each $100 bill will still be a $100 bill but, with 2% inflation, will only buy about half as much as when you buried it. What a waste.

Alternatively, you could use your savings to start a business—maybe singing, cutting hair, or writing software. However, you are probably not very good at crooning, clipping, or coding—that's why you chose a different job. Plus, how would you have time to do your current job well and also run a profitable business?

A better alternative is to invest in businesses that employ people who are actually good at singing songs, cutting hair, or writing software. If you lend them money at, say, an 8% interest rate, every $100 you lend will grow to more than $1000 after 30 years, which is a lot better than a buried $100 bill.

On the other hand, you are probably ill-equipped to evaluate borrowers and handle the paperwork involved in making loans and collecting loan payments. That's what banks are for. You might deposit money in a bank account paying, say, 4% interest and let the bank lend the money at 8% to borrowers it deems creditworthy. Each $100 you deposit will grow to $324 in 30 years—not as good as $1000 but still better than a buried $100 bill. Plus, your bank deposits are guaranteed by the federal government and you can withdraw your money whenever you want.

Another alternative is to invest in stocks issued by companies in the entertainment, grooming, or software industries. We mentioned earlier that stock investments have historically yielded, on average, more than 10% a year. A 10% return over 30 years will turn a $100 investment into $1745 after 30 years—the best option yet.

Whether you choose a loan, bank deposit, or newly issued stock, the consequences are the same: money is channeled from people like you who want to earn a return on their savings to people who want to buy things (like an automobile or house), start a business, or expand a business. Loans, banks, and stocks are not a sideshow, they are the main drivers of economic growth.

Without them, savers would have no good way of investing their savings and entrepreneurs would have no good way of financing their businesses.

Countries that do not have effective ways of channeling money from savers to entrepreneurs are much the poorer for it. In India, for example, hundreds of millions of people hoard silver and gold because they don't trust banks or the stock market and still believe that precious metals are real wealth. Only a third of the people in India have bank accounts; fewer own stocks or mutual funds. (In the U.S. the comparable numbers are 95% and 56%.)

This preference for hoarding precious metals has put a suffocating chokehold on the Indian economy. Not earning as much as they could on their savings, households have to save more in order to build their wealth. Not being able to borrow money easily, many families cannot buy homes and many entrepreneurs cannot start or expand their businesses. India is literally poorer for it.

Stock Exchanges

There is an important distinction between buying newly issued stock from a company and buying previously issued stock from other investors. Investors buy and sell many well-known stocks, such as Exxon and Wal-Mart, on the New York Stock Exchange (NYSE). Other stocks, such as Apple and Costco, are traded on the NASDAQ exchange. Either way, when you buy shares of Exxon or Apple on an exchange, you are buying shares from other investors, not from the company.

Even though the money you use to buy stock from other investors doesn't go to the company, the stock market is still important for channeling money from savers to entrepreneurs. When a new company first sells stock through an initial public offering (IPO) or when an established company sells additional stock, potential purchasers would be reluctant to invest if there was no way that they could ever sell the stock. They count on being able to sell on the NYSE or other exchanges if they ever need money or if they change their mind about owning shares in this company.

Stock exchanges have other effects on the economy. If a company is poorly managed, the price of its stock will crater, tempting others to buy enough stock to gain control of the company, replace the top management, and do a better job. This threat incentivizes managers to protect their jobs by doing their jobs well. In addition, management compensation is often directly tied to their company's stock price. The better they run the company, the better the chances that the stock price will increase and their compensation will increase. Again, the stock market has real effects on the economy.

The Stock Market Is the Main Show

The financial system in general and the stock market in particular are invaluable to modern economies. Where would we be without financial markets? The one thing we know for certain is that we would be a lot worse off. The stock market is not just a wild-and-crazy sideshow. It is the main show.

In the chapters to come, we will trace the evolution of investing over the centuries—from Investing 1.0 to 2.0 and all the way to the currently popular approach we call Investing 5.0. Our goal is to convince you that, not only should you invest in stocks (and other income-producing assets), but you should invest in a sensible, rational way. We want you to be aware of Investing 1.0 to 5.0 so that you can understand why there is a better way—what we call Investing 6.0. This approach is simple enough for anyone to use. No fancy math, complicated computer algorithms, or long hours are required. All you need are a few key principles and a healthy dose of common sense.

1

Investing 1.0—Blind Faith and Speculation

The early days of stock investing were characterized by little more than speculators guessing whether stock prices were about to go up or down—a fertile field for bubbles, panics, and market manipulation.

Stock trading began in 1600 when the British government gave the East India Company a royal charter to sail to the Indian Ocean and trade for spices, silk, and other luxuries. The voyages were risky because of the rough seas, pirates, and battles with Dutch and Portuguese trading ships. The East India Company was a *joint-stock company*, which meant that it was owned jointly by its stockholders, who received dividends from the company's trading profits. Modern corporations are also joint-stock companies but have the added bonus that the stockholders' liability is limited to the amount they invest.

Suppose, for example, that a company raises $1.5 million to open a restaurant: $1 million from selling 1 million shares of stock at $1 a share and $500,000 from a bank loan with an 8% interest rate. If the restaurant is successful and repays the loan, any additional profits belong to the shareholders, though the company may decide to use some of its profits to open more restaurants. If, on the other hand, the company falters and cannot repay its loan, the bank is entitled to whatever assets the company has and the stockholders get nothing more than an expensive lesson about the riskiness of restaurants. However (and this is an important however), the stockholders have limited liability in that they are not personally responsible for repaying the bank loan.

Two years after the British government chartered the East India Company, the Dutch government established the United East India Company as a corporation with limited liability. Its shares were traded on the Amsterdam Stock Exchange, which made it the first publicly traded company and, for many years, it was the only stock traded on the Amsterdam Exchange.

The British East India Company turned out to be very successful, establishing trading posts in India, Southeast Asia, Hong Kong, and the Persian Gulf. For more than 100 years, from 1757 to 1858, the East India Company controlled large parts of India. In 1858, the British Crown took control of India. The Dutch East India Company was also wildly successful, valued at its peak at $8 trillion in today's dollars.

The South Sea Bubble

A British company named the South Sea Company had a similar beginning but a different ending. The South Sea Company was founded in 1711 with the British government granting it exclusive trading rights in South America. The not-so-slight problem was that Spain and Portugal controlled most of South America—and England was at war with Spain. The South Sea Company had no real trading prospects unless the war ended and Spain granted substantial concessions to Britain. The war ended in 1713, but Spain's concessions were minimal.

Undaunted, the South Sea Company generated cash by selling more stock and propped up its stock price by lending money to people who bought shares at ever higher prices. In 1720, the Company audaciously agreed to take over Britain's national debt even though it had no plausible way of paying the interest due on the debt other than by selling more stock.

Nonetheless, encouraged by the government's evident faith in the South Sea Company and the company's inventive bookkeeping, the public rushed to buy shares. Figure 1.1 shows the sharp run-up in prices in the first six months of 1720. After languishing for nearly a decade, the company's stock price soared from £129 on January 29, 1720, to £199 on March 18, £400 on May 20, £770 on June 3, and £950 on June 29. Easy money! Stock prices were increasing so quickly that some said you could buy South Sea stock as you entered Garraway's Coffee House and sell it for a profit on the way out.

If people were eager to buy, swindlers were eager to sell. One company promised to build a perpetual motion machine—never mind that such a machine is impossible. Other companies were vague but the mystery may have added to the allure. One said that it was formed "for carrying on an undertaking of great advantage, but nobody is to know what it is." The company priced its shares at £100 each and promised an annual return of

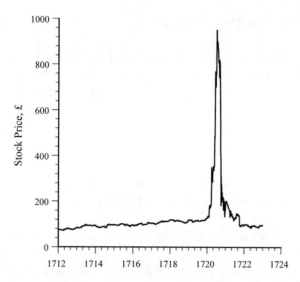

Fig. 1.1 The South Sea Company Bubble (*Credit* These data are from Larry Neal)

£100. The promotor sold all the shares in less than five hours, left England, and never returned. Another company described its business as "nitvender" or the selling of nothing. Yet, nitwits bought nitvender stock.

When the bubble ended, prices deflated as quickly as they had inflated. From its high of £950 in June, South Sea's stock price dropped to £400 on September 19 and £180 on September 28. By December, the price was back to where it had been before the madness began, down almost 90% from its peak.

The South Sea bubble now seems laughable but, at the time, it was easy to believe that stock prices would keep rising and fortunes would be made. When the bubble popped, dreams and fortunes vanished. In the spring of 1720, Sir Isaac Newton said, "I can calculate the motions of the heavenly bodies, but not the madness of people" and sold his South Sea shares for a £7000 profit ($1.5 million in 2023 dollars). Later that year, he bought shares again, just before the bubble burst, and lost £20,000 ($4.3 million in 2023 dollars). After James Milner, a member of the British Parliament, was bankrupted by the bubble, he explained, "I said, indeed, that ruin must soon come upon us but... it came two months sooner than I expected."

Hoping for Greater Fools

The South Sea Bubble is a good example of how early stock traders knew next to nothing about the stocks that were issued by legitimate businesses and clever scoundrels. Purchases and sales were based on little more than rumors, hunches, greed, and fear.

The enthusiastic purchase of dubious investments is fueled by the Greater Fool Theory:

Buy something at an inflated price with the hope that you can sell it to an even bigger fool at an even higher price.

For centuries, investing was haphazard speculation. Investors figured that a stock was worth whatever people were willing to pay, and the game was to guess what people will pay tomorrow for the stock you buy today. The great British economist, John Maynard Keynes, likened buying and selling stocks to childhood games:

it is, so to speak, a game of Snap, of Old Maid, of Musical Chairs — a pastime in which he is victor who says Snap neither too soon nor too late, who passes the Old Maid to his neighbour before the game is over, who secures a chair for himself when the music stops. These games can be played with zest and enjoyment, though all the players know that it is the Old Maid which is circulating, or that when the music stops some of the players will find themselves unseated.

Keynes explained how the key to winning the stock market game is to understand and anticipate one's opponents:

professional investment may be likened to those newspaper competitions in which the competitors have to pick out the six prettiest faces from a hundred photographs, the prize being awarded to the competitor whose choice most nearly corresponds to the average preferences of the competitors as a whole; so that each competitor has to pick, not those faces which he himself finds prettiest, but those which he thinks likeliest to catch the fancy of the other competitors, all of whom are looking at the problem from the same point of view. It is not a case of choosing those which, to the best of one's judgment, are really the prettiest, nor even those which average opinion genuinely thinks the prettiest. We have reached the third degree where we devote our intelligences to anticipating what average opinion expects the average opinion to be. And there are some, I believe, who practise the fourth, fifth and higher degrees.

The Greater Fool theory has fueled many a bubble—including the South Sea Bubble, Dutch Tulip Bubble, U.K. Bicycle Bubble, Japanese real estate bubble, dot-com bubble, and bitcoin bubble. Fools are prone to think that "this time is different" but it isn't.

The Building of a Bubble

Speculative bubbles generally begin with events of real economic significance, such as the building of railroads, discovery of gold, or invention of television. Early investors make profits and others rush to join the game, a self-fulfilling prophecy as the expanding demand pushes prices higher and gives speculators the profits they anticipated. Common sense gives way to greed and swindlers emerge to part fools from their money.

The elevated prices are a speculative bubble in that people are not buying an asset because they want to own it for many years and receive the income it generates but because they think they can sell the asset quickly to someone else for a higher price and a quick profit.

When the supply of greater fools dwindles, the bubble bursts and prices collapse. In the frantic rush for the exit, very few make it through the door.

Tulipmania

Like many bulb plants, Tulip bulbs multiply naturally, creating two to five more bulbs each growing cycle. After tulip bulbs were brought to Europe from Turkey in 1554, they quickly caught the fancy of European gardeners, especially wealthy Netherlanders who coveted bulbs that produced unusual flowers. As prices rose, speculators came to dominate trading and created the infamous bubble known as Tulipmania.

The lure is not difficult to understand. Buy a bulb and put it in the ground. At the end of the growing season, dig up several bulbs—each one of which can be sold for more than the cost of the first bulb. No wonder so many non-gardeners were buying and planting bulbs. Few paused to think about simple supply and demand. The annual multiplication of bulbs would eventually yield far more bulbs than real gardeners wanted to plant in their yards.

An added speculative wrinkle was that tulip bulbs must be in the ground from September until June, so people who bought bulbs did not have to pay for them until the bulbs were dug up in June. A speculator with little or no money could buy bulbs in September and sell them to a greater fool in October, thereby making a profit without ever paying for any bulbs. October fools could sell to November fools, and so on.

Serious gardeners made down payments and signed contracts witnessed by notaries. Speculators did neither, often making deals in taverns the way South Sea stocks were traded in English coffee houses. Figure 1.2 shows the launch of the tulip-price rocket ship in November 1636. A bulb that cost $25 (in 2023 dollars) in the summer of 1636 traded for $200 in January 1637 and $2500 a few weeks later. Some bulbs sold for $100,000; one was reportedly sold for more than a million dollars.

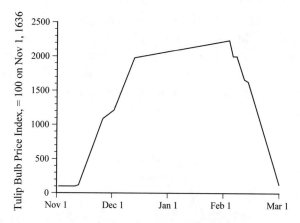

Fig. 1.2 Tulip Bulb Prices, November 1636 to March 1637

Then the bubble popped the way most bubbles end. Suddenly and unexpectedly, in February 1637, the market crashed virtually overnight. When prices started falling, buyers vanished since there is no point buying bulbs today that will be worth less (or, in some cases, *worthless*) tomorrow. In the absence of buyers, frantic sellers tried to get what they could for their bulbs.

Summer prices, when bulbs were harvested, were a tenth of what they had been in February. A century later, tulip prices were less than one-thousandth of the prices at the peak of Tulipmania.

The British Bicycle Bubble

Early bicycles came in a variety of sizes, shapes, and styles and were given colorful nicknames. The "dandy horse" had no pedals and was propelled by riders pushing their feet along the ground—essentially wheel-assisted walking. The "penny farthing" had pedals but the rider sat above a huge front wheel that dwarfed the tiny back wheel—similar to the size difference between the British penny and farthing coins. "Boneshaker" bicycles had iron-and-wood wheels which were ill-suited for rough terrain. What early bicycles had in common was that they were uncomfortable, unsafe, and expensive.

In the late 1800s, a series of technological innovations led to "safety bicycles" that had two identical wheels, a chain drive, a diamond frame, and inflatable tires. The British public embraced the safety, comfort, and cost of these improved bicycles. Middle class people who could not afford a horse or horse-and-carriage were able to travel conveniently through cities and far into the countryside—even over bad roads. Bicycles were also environmentally friendly in that they offered an inexpensive solution to what has become known as "the great horse manure crisis," a reference to the fact that the horses transporting people and goods were overwhelming cities with foul-smelling, disease-spreading horse droppings.

The number of British bicycle makers quintupled, from around 163 to 833. Many were financed by stock sales, with the number of publicly traded British companies producing cycles, tubes, or tires increasing from fewer than 10 in 1895 to 127 in 1897. At its peak, in 1896, British companies produced 750,000 bicycles a year, many of which were exported to the United States, France, and other countries that were similarly enamored with safety bicycles and clogged with horse manure.

As with many speculative stock bubbles, a genuine technological innovation led to rising stock prices that attracted speculators who expected prices to continue rising. Figure 1.3 shows that the stock prices of companies in the bicycle industry tripled during two months in 1896 while the overall British stock market languished.

Emotions trampled reason. During the tulip bulb bubble, the supply of bulbs increased because tulip bulbs multiply naturally. During the bicycle bubble, the sprouting of new companies increased the supply of bicycles, particularly, mass-produced American bicycles that cost 50% less than handmade British cycles. Enthusiasts shrugged off concerns about the rapidly increasing supply and gushed about a future in which bicycles would be the dominant form of transportation. Bicycles *were* revolutionary, but stock prices had become uncoupled from the profits of bicycle makers. Fools pointed to the revolution wrought by bicycles and the superior quality of

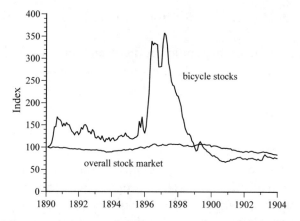

Fig. 1.3 The Bicycle Bubble (*Credit* These data are from Michael Quinn)

British bicycles, but the supply of greater fools dried up as the supply of bicycles erupted.

Figure 1.3 shows that stock prices of bicycles makers raced to a peak in 1897 and then fell 73% over the next few years. The bicycle bubble was different from the tulip bubble and South Sea bubble in that there was not a sudden pop but, instead, a gradual deflation, not unlike air slowly leaking out of a bicycle tire.

The Roaring Twenties

After the end of the brutality of World War I, the 1920s were a time of celebration and revolution in music, fashion, and the economy. Telephones, radios, movies, automobiles, and airplanes became widely available. The economic growth and prosperity were understandably reflected in stock prices. Companies were more profitable and people had more money to invest in stocks but rising stock prices lured in speculators looking for quick profits and counting on greater fools.

The Dow Jones Industrial Average surged past 100 in 1924, hitting 200 in December of 1927, 250 in October of 1928 and 300 in December. Nine months later, in September 1929, it reached a peak of 381. These companies were not nitvenders. The Dow is composed of strong, well-established blue chip companies. It seemed that anyone could get rich with little effort or risk simply by buying stock in well-known companies. American Can went from 77 to 182 between March 1928 and September 1929; American Telephone from 180 to 336, General Electric from 129 to 396, and U.S. Steel from 138 to 279.

Some people thought they could get rich even faster by giving their money to smart people who would make investments for them.

Ponzi Schemes

International reply coupons (IRCs) are international coupons that can be exchanged for the domestic postage stamps of countries that are members of the Universal Postal Union. IRCs allow people to send letters to persons living in foreign countries along with the postage required for a reply. IRCs are a thoughtful gesture but they were also the basis of the most famous swindle in history.

In 1920, there was a large difference between the official and open market exchange rate between Spanish pesos and U.S. dollars. Charles Ponzi, a Massachusetts man who had been through multiple prison terms and failed business ventures, devised a scheme for using IRCs to profit from this exchange-rate discrepancy. His plan was to use U.S. dollars to buy Spanish pesos at low prices in the open market, use these pesos to buy IRCs in Spain, and then trade these coupons for U.S. postage stamps in the United States at the higher official exchange rate. Not counting the logistics involved, he would purportedly buy 10 cents worth of U. S. postage stamps for a penny. It wasn't clear how he would sell these stamps (on card tables outside U. S. Post offices?) but such details did not seem to matter.

Ponzi raised money for his scheme by promising investors a 50% return every 45 days. Compounded eight times a year, the annual rate of return would be 2,463 percent! No wonder that he was able to raise $15 million (the equivalent of $230 million in 2023 dollars).

However, Ponzi seems to have bought only $61 in IRCs. His real plan was not to set up a private post office but to pay early investors with the money he received from later investors. Suppose someone invests $100, which Ponzi spends on himself. If Ponzi now finds two people to invest $100 apiece, he can give the initial investor $150, and keep $50 for himself. Now, he has 45 days to find four people willing to invest $100, so that he can pay each of the two previous investors $150 and spend $100 on himself. These four can be paid with the money from eight new suckers, and these eight from sixteen more.

This scam is now known as a *Ponzi scheme*. In a Ponzi scheme, money from new investors is paid to earlier ones, and it works as long as there are enough new investors. The problem is that the required number of fools grows surprisingly fast. The 21st round requires a million new fools and the 30th round requires a billion more. At some point, the scheme runs out of fools and those in the last round (the majority of the investors) are left with nothing. A Ponzi scheme merely transfers wealth from late entrants to early entrants (and to the person running the scam).

Ponzi's IRC scam collapsed after eight months when a Boston newspaper discovered that during the time that Ponzi supposedly bought $15 million in IRCs, the total amount sold worldwide came to only $1 million. Ponzi promised that he would repay his investors by starting a new company and selling stock to other investors—yep, another Ponzi scheme. Massachusetts officials apparently recognized it as such and sent Ponzi to jail for ten years.

Ponzi wasn't the only charlatan peddling swindles in the Roaring 20s. In Chicago, Leo Koretz sold stock in one company that was said to own rice plantations in Arkansas and another company that supposedly owned millions of acres of timberland and oil fields in Panama. The profits were so large that some investors jokingly referred to Kortz as "our Ponzi."

The joke was on them. It really was a Ponzi scheme, far larger and longer-lasting than the original. After a group of investors traveled to Panama and discovered the hoax, Koretz fled to Nova Scotia. Arrested there and returned to Chicago, he died in an Illinois prison.

Market Manipulation

The Roaring 20s were also marked by rampant stock market manipulation. With no way of gauging what stocks were really worth, investors often followed the herd—buying whichever stocks were going up in price, with no regard for a company's business or profits—a myopic behavior that creates opportunities for swindlers. In a *pump-and-dump* scheme, a group of scammers circulate fake rumors about a stock, while trading it back and forth among themselves at ever higher prices, luring in the credulous. After the price has been pumped up, the conspirators dump their holdings by selling to the suckers.

One notorious example involved the Radio Corporation of America—a 1920s-style high-tech company that manufactured and sold radio equipment and operated the NBC radio network. Like most speculative bubbles, there was a good story and plenty of hype—aided and abetted by a group of investors known as the "Radio Pool," who pumped and dumped RCA stock. Figure 1.4 shows how the price spurted from $53 on March 9, 1927, to $461 two years later, before crashing to less than $5.

The hustlers got out before the crash and pocketed $10 million for their chicanery. At the time, pump-and-dump schemes were legal. They were outlawed in the 1930s but there still are fraudsters who pump-and-dump flimsy stocks, cryptocurrencies, and other dodgy investments. Rising prices and smooth-talking promotors are good reasons for caution.

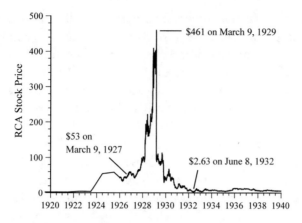

Fig. 1.4 The RCA Pump-and-Dump

The Crash

Predicting the future is always treacherous and history is full of well-informed people making what, with hindsight, were foolish statements. In 1899, the Director of the U.S. Patent Office said, "Everything that can be invented has been invented." Thomas Edison believed, "The phonograph is not of any commercial value" and President Rutherford Hayes said of the telephone: "That's an amazing invention, but who would ever want to use one?" Lord Kelvin, a scientist and president of Britain's Royal Society proclaimed, "Heavier than air flying machines are impossible" and Harry Warner, the president of Warner Brothers said, "Who the hell wants to hear actors talk?".

The stock market and the economy are never easy to predict and the Crash and Great Depression were no exception. In his final message to Congress, on December 4, 1928, Calvin Coolidge boasted, "No Congress of the United States ever assembled, on surveying the state of the Union, has met with a more pleasing prospect than that which appears at the present time." Herbert Hoover took office in March of 1929 and in July boasted, "The outlook of the world today is for the greatest era of commercial expansion in history." On October 17, 1929, Irving Fisher, the greatest American economist of his day, asserted that stocks had reached "what looks like a permanently high plateau."

Figure 1.5 shows that the five-year bull market was over and Fisher could not have been more wrong. After a number of bad days, panic selling hit the market on Thursday, October 24. Terrified investors tried to sell at any price and market prices plunged, with the panic heightened by the fact that the ticker tape reporting transactions ran hours late, so that investors had no information about current prices. The market finally steadied in the afternoon when six prominent New York bankers put up $40 million apiece to buy stocks. But the market dropped again the following Monday and was hit by panic selling the next day, Black Tuesday, October 29th. There was another avalanche of sell orders, more than the brokers and ticker tape could process, and dwarfing the scattered buy orders. White Sewing Machine had recently traded for $48. On Monday it closed at $11. On Black Tuesday, in the complete absence of buy orders, a messenger boy bought shares for $1.

With fits and starts, the market collapse continued. By November 13, the Dow had fallen an incredible 48% as the prices of America's premier companies collapsed: American Can was down 53%, American Telephone 41%, General Electric 58%, and U.S. Steel 46%. But Hoover's optimism persisted. In his December 3, 1929, State of the Union message, he concluded, "The problems with which we are confronted are the problems of growth and progress." In March 1930, both President Hoover and the Secretary of Commerce predicted that business would be normal by May. In early May, Hoover declared that "we have now passed the worst." In late May, he predicted recovery by the fall. In June, he told a group that had come to Washington to urge increased government spending, "Gentlemen, you have come sixty days too late. The depression is over."

The President's cheerleading did not reassure investors. In October, the Republican National Chairman complained that "persons high in Republican circles are beginning to believe that there is some concerted effort on foot

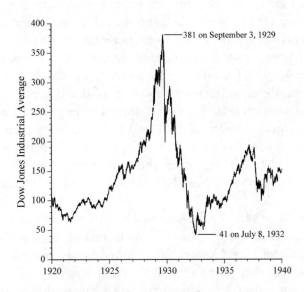

Fig. 1.5 The Roaring Twenties and the Great Crash

to utilize the stock market as a method of discrediting the administration. Every time an administration official gives out an optimistic statement about business conditions, the market immediately drops."

The Dow recovered to nearly 300 in the spring of 1930, but then began a long, tortuous slide, punctuated by brief rallies before finally touching bottom at 41.22 in July of 1932—down 89% from its September 1929 peak. It wasn't until 1956, 27 years later, that the stock market regained its 1929 level.

The Great Depression was more than a stock market crash. Between 1929 and 1933, U.S. GDP fell by a third, while the unemployment rate rose from 3 to 25%. More than a third of the nation's banks failed and household wealth dropped by 30%. Behind these aggregate numbers were millions of private tragedies. One hundred thousand businesses failed and twelve million people lost their jobs, and, with them, their income and self-respect. Many lost their life savings in the stock market crash and the tidal wave of bank failures. Without income or savings, people could not buy food, clothing, or proper medical care. Those who could not pay their rent lost their shelter; those who could not make mortgage payments lost their homes. Farm income fell by two-thirds and many farms were lost to foreclosure. Desperate people moved into shanty settlements (called Hoovervilles); slept under newspapers (Hoover blankets); and scavenged for food where they could.

The unemployment rate averaged 19% during the 1930s and never fell below 14%. The Great Depression didn't end until the federal government began spending nearly $100 billion a year during World War II.

The Aftermath

During the Investing 1.0 period, financial markets played an important role in the economic growth of America and many ordinary people bought stocks. However, Investing 1.0 was also marked by ill-informed investment decisions, booms and busts, bubbles and crashes, blind faith and speculation, Ponzi schemes, and market manipulation.

After the Great Crash, millions of people left the stock market and vowed they would never return. Later generations who did not experience the crash firsthand did not absorb the lessons that might have been learned about the perils of an Investing 1.0 mindset. It is hard to resist the lure of quick riches and many succumb. In Chapter 4, we will discuss two recent examples of the perils of Investing 1.0 thinking—the dot-com and cryptocurrency bubbles.

A positive aftereffect of the Great Crash was that serious people began thinking seriously about how to make rational investment decisions based on more than greed, fear, and uninformed guesses about the direction stock prices might go next. Investing 2.0 brought logic and rationality to investing.

References

Carswell, John. 1960. *The South Sea Bubble*, London: Cresset Press.
Dunn, Donald H. 1975. *Ponzi: The Boston Swindler*, New York: McGraw-Hill.
Garber, Peter M. 1989. Tulipmania, *Journal of Political Economy*, 97(3), 535–60.
Keynes, John Maynard. 1936. *The General Theory of Employment, Interest, and Money*, New York: Macmillan, Chapter 12.
Kindleberger, Charles P. 1978. *Manias, Panics, and Crashes*, New York: Basic Books.
Powell, James. 2021. Men of Leisure Deflated by the Great Bicycle Bubble, *Financial Times*, December 13.
Quinn, William, and Turner, John D. 2021. Riding the Bubble or Taken for a Ride? Investors in the British Bicycle Mania, November 1. https://ssrn.com/abstract=3954390 or https://doi.org/10.2139/ssrn.3954390.

2

Investing 2.0—The Birth of Value Investing

During the many decades of Investing 1.0, there was little rhyme or reason behind investment decisions. Speculative guesses about whether a stock's price was about to go up or down were fertile ground for the Greater Fool Theory. Then the carnage left by the Great Crash gave rise to two visionaries, John Burr Williams and Benjamin Graham, who moved investment analysis from Investing 1.0 to Investing 2.0 by arguing that investors can estimate what stocks are really worth.

After studying mathematics and chemistry at Harvard and earning an MBA from the Harvard Business School, Williams worked as a security analysis during the 1920s and the subsequent crash. In 1932 he returned to Harvard for a PhD in economics. His ambitious thesis, *The Theory of Investment Value*, was intended to set forth "a new sub-science… that shall comprise a coherent body of principles like the theory of Money and the Theory of International Trade." Notice the title was not "A Theory" but "The Theory." Williams struggled to find a publisher for his dissertation because it contained mathematical equations and algebraic symbols. Harvard eventually published it in 1938, though Williams had to pay part of the printing costs.

When investors value bonds, loans, apartment buildings, and businesses, they think about the income they can anticipate receiving from their investment. In the same way, Williams argued that, instead of trying to predict ups and downs in a stock's price, investors should focus their attention on the income they receive from the stock—the dividends. The relevant question is the amount you would be willing to pay in order to receive the dividends without ever selling the stock. That amount is the stock's *intrinsic value*. People who think this way are called *value investors*.

One of legendary investor Warren Buffett's aphorisms is, "My favorite holding period is forever." If we think this way, never planning to sell, we force ourselves to value stocks based on the cash they generate, instead of being distracted by guesses about future zigs and zags in stock prices.

The idea is simple and powerful, but often elusive. It is very hard to buy a stock without looking at what its price has been in the past and thinking about what its price might be in the future. It is very hard to think about waiting patiently for dividends to accumulate, when it is so tempting to think about making a quick killing by flipping stocks. Above all else, value investing requires discipline.

While Williams was writing for academics, Benjamin Graham wrote his masterpiece, *Security Analysis*, in 1934 for professional investors—indeed, it became known as the "Bible of Wall Street." He later published a more accessible version titled, *The Intelligent Investor*.

Graham was fluent in Greek and Latin and, after graduating from Columbia University in 1914, was offered jobs teaching English, math, and philosophy there. Instead, he worked on Wall Street. He eventually agreed to teach an investment class at the Columbia Business School if the university would provide a reliable notetaker. A young assistant professor named David Dodd volunteered and his notes turned into their co-authored book, *Security Analysis*.

Graham's parents lost their savings in the Bank Panic of 1907. Graham made a fortune buying stocks in the 1920s and lost it during the Great Crash. The lessons he drew were that, instead of speculating about fluctuations in stock prices, investors should study a company's balance sheets looking for assets, earnings, and dividends.

One big difference between Williams and Graham was that Williams focused on a company's future dividends while Graham emphasized current earnings and assets. However, Williams knew that earnings and assets are the source of dividends and Graham considered a solid history of dividend payments to be evidence of a company's financial strength.

The Intrinsic Value of an Investment

The central principle of value investing is that, instead of trying to predict changes in stock prices, investors should focus on a company's assets, earnings, and dividends. Thus, Williams wrote that sensible people buy

> *A cow for her milk*
> *A hen for her eggs*
> *And a stock, by heck*
> *For her dividends.*
> *An orchard for fruit*
> *Bees, for their honey*
> *And stock, besides,*
> *For their dividends.*

It would be a mistake "to buy a cow for her cud or bees for their buzz."

The very first sentence of Williams's *Theory of Investment Value* is, "Separate and distinct things not to be confused, as every thoughtful investor knows, are real worth and market price." If a city slicker comes to your farm and offers a low price for your cow, you ignore him. You bought the cow for the milk, not to sell to city slickers. If the city slicker returns the next day and offers a ridiculously high price, more than the value of a cow's lifetime of milk, you take advantage of his ignorance.

In the same way, Graham created an imaginary Mr. Market, a person who comes by every day offering to buy the stock you own or to sell you more shares. Mr. Market's price is sometimes reasonable and, other times, silly. There is no reason for your assessment of a stock's value to be swayed by Mr. Market's prices, though you may sometimes take advantage of his foolishness.

The Investing 2.0 strategy is to compare a stock's intrinsic value to its current market price.

The Present Value of Dividends

In order to estimate a stock's intrinsic value, John Burr Williams argued that investors should think about how much they would be willing to pay to receive the anticipated dividends from the stock—with no expectation of ever selling. This mindset forces investors to think about the cash generated by companies instead of guessing whether a stock's price tomorrow will be higher or lower than its price today.

To illustrate this approach, consider a stock that will pay a $10 dividend every year, beginning one year from today. (Companies generally pay dividends quarterly; for simplicity, we assume annual dividends.) How much would you pay for something that gives you $10 every year, forever?

The amount you would be willing to pay—the intrinsic value—needs to take into account the fact that a $10 dividend received one year from now is not as valuable as having $10 today because, if you have $10 now, you can invest it and it will be worth more than $10 one year from now. A $10 dividend $10 two years from is even less valuable. The value today of money received in the future is called the *present value*. A stock's intrinsic value is the total present value of all its future dividends.

The mathematical formula for the present value V of annual dividends, D_1, D_2, and so on, is

$$V = \frac{D_1}{(1+R)^1} + \frac{D_2}{(1+R)^2} + \frac{D_3}{(1+R)^3} + \ldots \qquad (2.1)$$

where R is your *required rate of return*. In our example, the annual dividends are a constant $10 and we will assume a 10% required return:

$$V = \frac{\$10}{(1+0.10)^1} + \frac{\$10}{(1+0.10)^2} + \frac{\$10}{(1+0.10)^3} + \ldots$$

If the required return is 10 percent, then the present value of a $10 dividend paid one year from today is $9.09 because $9.09 invested for one year at 10% will grow to $10. Similarly, the present value of a $10 dividend two years from today is $8.26 because $8.26 invested for two years at 10% will grow to $10. The intrinsic value of this stock is the sum of the present values of each $10 dividend:

$$V = \frac{\$10}{(1+0.10)^1} + \frac{\$10}{(1+0.10)^2} + \frac{\$10}{(1+0.10)^3} + \ldots$$

$$= \$9.09 + \$8.26 + \$7.51 + \ldots$$

The lower line in Fig. 2.1 shows that the value of each annual $10 dividend inexorably declines the longer we have to wait to receive it. A $10 dividend is only worth $1.49 if we have to wait 20 years for it and $0.22 if we have to wait 40 years.

The upper line in Fig. 2.1 shows the cumulative value. The first dividend is worth $9.09 and the second is worth $8.26, a cumulative value of $9.09 + $8.26 = $17.35. As the value of distant dividends approaches 0, the cumulative value converges to $100.

Consols

An investment that pays a constant amount forever is called a *perpetuity* or a *consol*, so named because the British government consolidated its debts in

2 Investing 2.0—The Birth of Value Investing

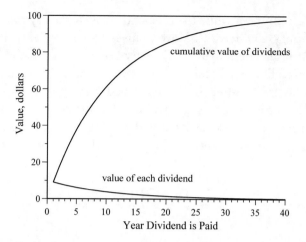

Fig. 2.1 Present value of $10 annual dividends

1751 (and in later years) by issuing bonds with constant payments and no maturation date. The government did, however, reserve the right to redeem the bonds and change the size of the annual payments, which it did several times before redeeming the last of its consols in 2015. The U.S. government has also issued consol bonds in the past but these, too, have all been redeemed.

Academics love consols because the present value formula in Eq. 2.1 simplifies to

$$V = \frac{D}{R}$$

In our example, the annual dividend is $10 and the required return is 10%, so the present value is $100,

$$V = \frac{D}{R} = \frac{\$10}{0.10} = \$100$$

which is confirmed by the cumulative-dividend line in Fig. 2.1. This makes sense. If you buy a stock for $100 that pays a $10 annual dividend forever, then you are indeed receiving a 10% return.

Williams called the required rate of return R for a stock an investor's "personal rate of interest." An investor's required return surely depends on the returns available on other investments, such as Treasury bonds. Suppose that the interest rate on Treasury bonds is 5%. Stocks are riskier than Treasury bonds because the annual payments that Treasury bonds make are guaranteed by the U.S. government while the dividends that stocks pay can be predicted but are far from guaranteed. Risk-averse investors consequently have a higher required return on stocks than on Treasury bonds. How much higher? If the interest rate on Treasury bonds is 5%, would you be satisfied with a 12% return from stocks? Most likely. What about 10%? Or 8%? It's your call.

The consul formula makes it easy to calculate the effect of changes in required returns. If interest rates fall and your required return dips from 10 to 5%, then the intrinsic value of a $10 annual dividend increases from $100 to $200:

$$V = \frac{D}{R} = \frac{\$10}{0.05} = \$200$$

This again makes sense. Paying $200 for a stock that pays $10 a year forever gives you a 5% return.

Investors do not apply the same required return to all investments, because some investments are riskier than others. If Treasury bonds pay 5%, you may well require a 20%, 30%, or even higher return on shaky promises. The riskier the investment, the higher is the required return and the lower its present value.

Valuing Growth

We can use a slightly more complicated, but still simple, valuation equation for a stock (or any other asset) whose income grows at a constant rate forever. John Burr Williams showed that the present value formula in Eq. 2.1 now simplifies to this equation (which we label with his initials, JBW):

$$\text{JBW}: V = \frac{D}{R - g} \qquad (2.2)$$

(Myron J. Gordon popularized Williams' equation and it is often called the *Gordon growth model*.)

With an initial $10 dividend, a 10% required return, and a 4% dividend growth rate, the intrinsic value is $166.67:

$$V = \frac{\$10}{0.10 - 0.04} = \$166.67$$

Figure 2.2 shows the value of the annual and cumulative dividends. As before, the initial $10 dividend has a present value of $9.09. The second-year dividend is 4% higher, $10.40, which has a present value of $8.60, the third-year dividend is $10.82 and has a present value of $8.13. Even though the dividends are growing by 4% each year, the 10% discount rate inexorably diminishes their present value. As the present value of the distant dividends approaches zero, the cumulative present value approaches $166.67 (as given by the JBW equation):

$$V = \frac{\$10.00}{(1+0.10)^1} + \frac{\$10.40}{(1+0.10)^2} + \frac{\$10.82}{(1+0.10)^3} + \ldots$$
$$= \$9.09 + \$8.60 + \$8.15$$
$$= \$166.67$$

To recap: The correct way to think about a stock or other prospective investment is to consider the future income it will generate and then discount this income by a required return that takes into account the time value of money. This simple idea is the cornerstone of value investing.

The intrinsic value does not depend on predictions about what a stock's price will be tomorrow, a year from now, or 20 years from now. The only price that matters is today's price. A stock is worth buying if Mr. Market's price today is lower than the stock's intrinsic value. The bigger the gap, the bigger the appeal.

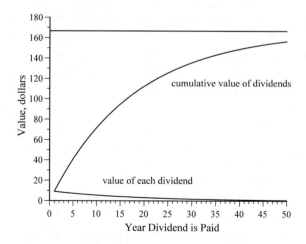

Fig. 2.2 Present value of dividends starting at $10 and increasing by 4% each year

Growth Matters (A Lot)

Dividends never grow at a perfectly constant rate, but the JBW equation is a reasonable approximation with logical implications. For example, the JBW equation demonstrates how important the growth rate is to the value of a stock. We have just seen that, with a 10% required return, a stock paying a $10 dividend has an intrinsic value of $100 if there is no growth and an intrinsic value of $166.67 with 4% growth.

Growth matters a lot because of the power of compounding. The difference between 0 and 4% growth may not sound like much; but 30 years from now, the first company will still be paying a $10 dividend while the second pays a $32.43 dividend. This reasoning explains why stocks that pay growing dividends are often far more valuable than bonds and other fixed-income investments that make annual payments that do not increase over time.

This logic also explains the lure of *growth* stocks—companies with high anticipated growth rates. The logic works in reverse, too. Sometimes, a company with bright prospects announces an earnings increase and its stock price free-falls downward. Why? Because the announced increase was not as big as had been anticipated, and small differences in growth rates can make a big difference to the value of a company's stock. In our example, a reduction in the anticipated growth rate from 4% to zero reduces the intrinsic value of the stock by 40%, from $166.67 to $100.

A particularly dramatic example happened to Oracle, a software powerhouse, on December 9, 1997. Analysts had been expecting Oracle's second-quarter sales to be 35% higher than a year earlier and its profits to be 25% higher. After the market closed on December 8, Oracle reported that its second-quarter sales were only 23% higher than a year earlier and its profits were only 4% higher. The next day, 171.8 million Oracle shares were traded, more than one-sixth of all Oracle shares outstanding, and the stock's price fell 29%, reducing Oracle's total market value by more than $9 billion.

Figure 2.3 shows that, as is so often the case, Mr. Market overreacted. A $10,000 investment in Oracle the day after its 1997 crash would have grown to $256,000 on December 31, 2022, compared to $63,000 for the S&P 500.

More recently, on January 23, 2013, Apple reported a record quarterly profit of $13.1 billion. It had sold 28% more iPhones and 48% more iPads than a year earlier, but the stock dropped more than 12%, reducing its market value by $50 billion. Apple had sold a record 47.8 million iPhones, but this was less than the consensus forecast of 50 million. Earnings per share were *higher* than forecasted ($13.81 vs $13.44), and so was revenue ($54.5 billion vs $54.7 billion), but investors were used to Apple clobbering forecasts. A bit

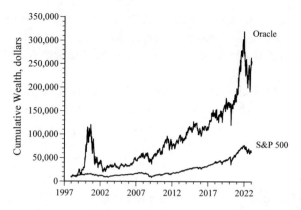

Fig. 2.3 A $10,000 investment in Oracle or the S&P 500 after Oracle crashed in 1997

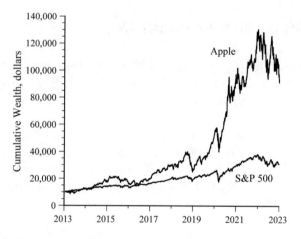

Fig. 2.4 A $10,000 investment in Apple or the S&P 500 after Apple crashed in 2013

of a paradox here: If analysts expect Apple to beat their forecasts, why don't they raise their forecasts? In any case, Mr. Market was scared and Apple's stock price plunged. This, too, proved to be an overreaction. Figure 2.4 shows that a $10,000 investment in Apple immediately after the January 24, 2013, crash would have been worth $94,000 on December 31, 2022, compared to $31,000 for the S&P500.

While the value of growth cannot be doubted, the uncertainty in valuing rapidly growing companies is what kept Ben Graham away from growth stocks. Thinking the same way, Warren Buffett has always had an aversion to speculative growth stocks and a fondness for boring companies that generate profits reliably: Benjamin-Moore, Burlington Northern, Dairy Queen, Fruit of the Loom, GEICO, See's Candy, Coca-Cola, Kraft, Procter & Gamble.

When Buffett bought Apple stock in 2016, this did not mean that he had changed his mind about growth stocks. Instead, it signaled that he now viewed Apple as a mature company with dependable profits and an attractive stock price.

There is an old Wall Street saying, "A bargain that stays a bargain isn't a bargain," suggesting that buying a stock at a low price is not a good investment if the price doesn't increase afterward. Value investors don't think this way. They are not dismayed if a stock's price doesn't go up, because they buy stocks for income, not price appreciation. In fact, if a stock's price drops and the income projections haven't changed, they will buy more. In market panics, value investors say, "Wall Street is having a sale." They back up a truck and fill it with bargains.

Are Stocks a Ponzi Scheme? Nope

In 2020 Tim Denning, a writer for CNBC and Business Insider, wrote an article with the provocative title, "The Stock Market Is a Ponzi Scheme." It was inspired by a "financial expert" named Tan Lui, who argued,

> *The simple truth is profits from buying and selling stocks come from other investors who are buying and selling stocks. When someone buys low and sells high, another sucker is also buying high and needs to sell for even higher. Companies like Google, Amazon, and Tesla never pay their shareholders. Their investors' profits are dependent on the inflow of money from new investors, which by definition, is how a Ponzi scheme works.*

Liu concludes that "$34 trillion of stock value = $0 in real money." The irony here is that stocks are generally the antithesis of a Ponzi scheme. The defining characteristic of a Ponzi scheme is that there are no profitable assets, so the only way investors can make money is by taking money from new investors. Profitable companies, in contrast, have assets that generate income that they can give to their stockholders without recruiting new investors.

Liu had been a bike courier and freelance photojournalist before he began working in finance. Suppose that he had started a small courier business, Liu Delivers, and was married at the time, with his spouse working in finance and paying their living expenses. Suppose, too, that Liu Delivers was reliably profitable, but Liu didn't take any money out of the business. Instead, he repaid the loan he used to get started and then advertised, hired more couriers, and put in a modern billing system—and his profits increased at a double-digit rate year after year. Is Liu Delivers a Ponzi scheme because it doesn't pay dividends? Hardly. Liu Delivers is valuable because it generates substantial income, unlike a Ponzi scheme that merely shuffles cash among investors.

What if Liu had shareholders? Would that make Liu Delivers a Ponzi scheme? Nope. Liu Delivers might pay dividends at some point, or Liu Delivers might be sold to another company but that hardly matters. The intrinsic value of Liu Delivers comes from the company's profitability.

Now consider Berkshire Hathaway. Berkshire doesn't pay dividends so, by Liu's criterion, it is a Ponzi scheme. Yet, Berkshire owns lots of companies that do pay dividends. For example, as of July 2023, Berkshire owned 916 million shares of Apple stock, which were valued at roughly $175 billion and paid Berkshire $880 million in annual dividends. Apple is not a Ponzi scheme, so how can it turn into a Ponzi scheme when its stock is purchased by Berkshire? It makes no sense, because Liu's argument is nonsensical.

Finally, suppose that Liu Delivers had been a Ponzi scheme that didn't have any income at all but sold more stock every year, using the proceeds to pay dividends to its shareholders. It would be a Ponzi scheme even though it pays dividends. It is not the presence or absence of dividends that determine whether something is a Ponzi scheme. It is the presence or absence of real profits.

The overwhelming majority of U.S. corporations are profitable businesses and, unlike Ponzi schemes, they have been and will continue to be worthwhile investments (if the stock prices are reasonable).

The Dividend Yield

There are a variety of value-investing benchmarks for assessing whether stock prices are reasonable. One simple metric is the dividend yield, D/P, the ratio of the current annual dividend to the price,

$$\text{dividend yield} = \frac{\text{annual dividend}}{\text{price}}$$

Suppose, for simplicity, that a stock pays annual dividends and that the next dividend will be $2, paid one year from today. If the current stock price is $100, then the dividend yield is 2%:

$$\frac{D}{P} = \frac{\$2}{\$100}$$
$$= 0.02. (2\%)$$

If the dividend never grew and stayed at $2 forever, then receiving a $2 dividend every year is clearly a 2% return on a $100 investment. However, most firms grow with the economy and their earnings and dividends grow, too.

With, say, a 5% growth rate, the dividend is $2.00 one year from now, $2.10 the next year, $2.21 the year after that, and so on. Incredibly, the JBW equation tells us that if we replace the intrinsic value V with the market price P in Eq. 2.2, we can estimate the investor's return by adding the dividend growth rate to the dividend yield: 2% + 5% = 7%.

$$R = \frac{D}{P} + g$$
$$= \frac{\$2}{\$100} + 0.05$$
$$= 0.02 + 0.05$$
$$= 0.07$$

One way to think about this is that, other things being equal, Eq. 2.2 implies that the value of a stock increases at the same rate as its dividends, here 5%. So, an annual 2% dividend and 5% increase in intrinsic value gives a 7% total return. We can then compare this benchmark stock return to the returns on Treasury bonds and other investments.

Figure 2.5 shows the history of the S&P 500 dividend yield and the interest rate on 10-year Treasury bonds. It is striking that, up until the 1950s, the dividend yield was generally well above the Treasury rate. In 1950, for example, stocks had a dividend yield of nearly 9%, when long-term Treasury rates were only 2%. Investors evidently woefully underestimated the likelihood that dividends would grow over time, providing double-digit returns from stocks compared to a 2% return from bonds. What a great time to be a value investor!

Things changed in the late 1950s, when interest rates exceeded dividend yields until they converged in 2009. Remember that the benchmark return estimate is the dividend yield *plus* the dividend growth rate. As we are writing this in July 2023, the interest rate on 10-year Treasury bonds is 4.06% and the S&P 500 dividend yield is 1.56%. The benchmark long-run return on stocks exceeds that on bonds for any dividend growth rate above 2.50%:

$$R = \frac{D}{P} + g$$
$$= 0.0156 + 0.0250$$
$$= 0.0406$$

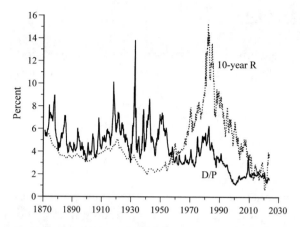

Fig. 2.5 The S&P 500 dividend yield D/P and 10-year Treasury rate R, 1871–2023

Other Income Measures

Value investors use a variety of other metrics in the John Burr Williams tradition. For example, some people estimate a company's free cash flow (FCF), which measures the cash a firm has available to pay dividends to its stockholders and to pay interest on its bonds and other debts. Others estimate a company's economic value added (EVA), which is the difference between what a company earns and what its earnings would be if the company's profit rate were equal to the shareholders' required rate of return.

The details are more complicated than forecasting dividends but FCF and EVA both have the advantage of being able to estimate the intrinsic value of companies that do not pay dividends. Their validity is confirmed by the fact that when the FCF and EVA models are applied to companies that do pay dividends, they give the same intrinsic value estimates as does the JBW dividend-discount equation.

The Earnings Yield

One popular benchmark is a stock's price-earnings ratio, P/E, which is obtained by dividing the price per share by the annual earnings per share:

$$P/E = \frac{\text{price}}{\text{annual earnings}}$$

A high P/E for an individual stock or for a market index like the S&P 500 signals that it is expensive.

Ben Graham once separated the thirty Dow Jones stocks into the ten stocks with the highest P/E ratios, the ten middle stocks, and the ten lowest. For every five-year holding period between 1937 and 1969, the low P/E stocks outperformed the middle P/E stocks, which outperformed the high P/E stocks. If $10,000 had been invested and reinvested every five years in the ten stocks with the lowest P/E ratios, this investment would have been worth over $100,000 in 1969, more than twice the value of a recurring investment in the ten highest P/E stocks. More recent studies have come to a similar conclusion.

Figure 2.6 shows that the price-earnings ratio for the S&P 500 has varied considerably, falling close to 5 in some years and topping 20 in others. The average value has been 16.0. (Fig. 2.6 omits several months in 2009 when the P/E went above 100 because earnings collapsed and stock prices did not fall as far as earnings because investors believed that the recession would not last long.)

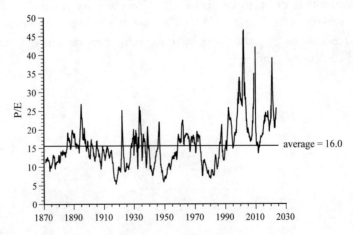

Fig. 2.6 The S&P 500 price-earnings ratio, 1871–2023

Although P/E ratios are suggestive, a low P/E is not necessarily a bargain and a high P/E is not necessarily a bubble. There are rational reasons why one stock might be expensive even though its P/E is low and another stock might be a bargain even though its P/E is high. Remember that the intrinsic value of a stock depends on the income it is expected to generate in the *future*. Growth stocks tend to have relatively high P/Es because their future earnings are expected to be much larger than current earnings.

Intrinsic values also depend on the interest rates used to discount future income: high interest rates reduce intrinsic values and should reduce P/Es too. A convenient way to see this relationship between interest rates and P/Es is to calculate the earnings yield, E/P, which is the inverse of the P/E ratio.

$$\text{earnings yield} = \frac{E}{P} = \frac{\text{annual earnings}}{\text{price}}$$

The earning yield is a rough estimate of the shareholders' return on their stock. If a stock sells for $100 a share and the company earns $10 a share, then the earnings yield is 10%:

$$\text{earnings yield} = \frac{\text{annual earnings}}{\text{price}}$$
$$= \frac{\$10}{\$100}$$
$$= 0.10\ (10\%)$$

The earnings yield isn't necessarily equal to the shareholders' return because stockholders receive dividends, not earnings. Earnings are the source of dividends but they are the means to an end, not the end. Suppose a company pays a $2 dividend out of $10 in earnings per share and retains $8, which it squanders on an ill-advised misadventure. The squandered $8 may as well have never existed.

For a dollar of retained earnings to be worth a dollar to shareholders, the firm must earn a return equal to the shareholders' required return. A dollar of retained earnings is worth less than a dollar if the firm earns less than the required return and more than a dollar if the firm earns more than the required return. This is why Berkshire Hathaway doesn't pay dividends. Its managers believe that they can choose investments that earn more than their shareholders' required return.

Despite this important caveat, Fig. 2.7 shows that the earnings yield for the S&P 500 has generally gone up and down with the interest rate on 10-year Treasury bonds over the past 60 years.

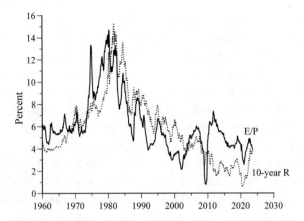

Fig. 2.7 The S&P 500 earnings yield E/P and 10-year Treasury rate R

Shiller's Cyclically Adjusted Earnings

Corporate earnings fluctuate as the economy surges and sags. Nobel laureate Robert Shiller has a sensible way of smoothing out these fluctuations. First, he calculates real, inflation-adjusted earnings each month for the S&P 500. Then, he calculates the average of these monthly inflation-adjusted earnings over the previous ten years. The cyclically adjusted price-earnings ratio (CAPE) is equal to the inflation-adjusted value of the S&P 500 divided by 10-year average of inflation-adjusted earnings.

$$\text{CAPE} = \frac{\text{price}}{\text{average earnings}}$$

We can also calculate the inverse, the cyclically adjusted earnings yield (CAEP):

$$\text{CAEP} = \frac{\text{average earnings}}{\text{price}}$$

CAEP is an estimate of the anticipated inflation-adjusted return on stocks so we should compare it to the anticipated inflation-adjusted return on bonds. Figure 2.8 uses the average rate of inflation over the previous 10 years to calculate the real, inflation-adjusted interest rate on 10-year Treasury bonds. This calculation assumes that the rate of inflation over the preceding 10 years is a reasonable estimate of expected future inflation.

CAEP has generally been well above inflation-adjusted interest rates, indicating that stocks have generally been a more promising investment than

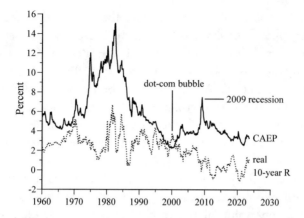

Fig. 2.8 The real 10-year Treasury rate and the cyclically adjusted earnings yield (CAEP)

Treasury bonds. Notice the exception, during the peak of the dot-com bubble in the second half of 1999 and the spring of 2000. As we write this in early July 2023, the inflation-adjusted earning yield on stocks (CAEP) is 3.24% and the inflation-adjusted interest rate on Treasury bonds is 1.11%. The spread between the two is 3.24% − 1.11% = 2.13%, which might persuade many value investors that stocks are a somewhat more attractive investment than Treasury bonds.

Figure 2.8 shows two noteworthy episodes in recent years. During the peak of the dot-com bubble in the spring of 2000, rising stock prices pulled CAEP 1.5 percentage points *below* the inflation-adjusted Treasury yield—suggesting that stocks were a relatively unattractive investment. During the 2009 recession, in contrast, falling stock prices pushed CAEP more than 7 percentage points *above* the inflation-adjusted Treasury yield—suggesting that stocks were very attractively priced. We will discuss these two historical episodes in more detail in later chapters.

An S&P 500 Valuation

On July 8, 2022, Gary wrote a MarketWatch column that used the JBW equation to estimate the intrinsic value of the S&P 500:

$$\text{JBW}: V = \frac{D}{R - g}$$

To do so, he took into account the fact that companies often repurchase some of their stock from shareholders. In his 2021 letter to Berkshire Hathaway shareholders, Warren Buffett noted that Berkshire had spent $51.7 billion during the past two years repurchasing 9% of Berkshire's shares. During that same period, Apple (46% of Berkshire's total stock portfolio at the time) repurchased more than $156 billion of its stock—described by Buffett as "an act we applaud." More broadly, the companies in the S&P 500 spent more than $5 trillion over the previous decade buying back shares.

Figure 2.9 shows that the amount of money distributed to shareholders through share repurchases has generally exceeded dividends in recent years.

By John Burr Williams' reasoning, the intrinsic value of a company's stock is the present value of the cash it gives its stockholders—no matter whether that cash is distributed through dividends or share repurchases. This reasoning is clearest if you imagine that you are the only shareholder and that you hold the stock forever. The total income you receive is the cash paid to you as dividends plus the cash paid to you to repurchase shares.

In theory, repurchases are equivalent to dividends and should be treated the same as dividends. In practice, taxes give share repurchases a clear advantage. Shareholders must pay taxes on dividends, but they don't pay taxes on stock sales unless the sale price is higher than the purchase price—and, even then, they only pay taxes on the capital gain (if any). A dividend gives shareholders no alternative but to take the cash and pay taxes. With a share repurchase, shareholders have a choice. They can either sell shares and (possibly) pay taxes on the capital gain, or they can let their investment ride.

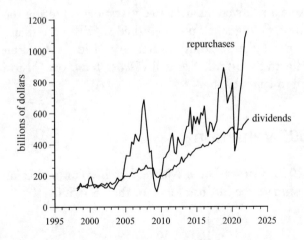

Fig. 2.9 S&P 500 dividends and share repurchases

2 Investing 2.0—The Birth of Value Investing

A second difference is that corporations might repurchase their shares because they feel that Mr. Market has priced the stock at less than its intrinsic value, making repurchases a hot deal—the same as if the company were to acquire another company at a discounted price. If, however, Mr. Market's price is too high, then share repurchases are a bad deal. Thus, Buffett wrote,

> I want to underscore that for Berkshire repurchases to make sense, our shares must offer appropriate value. We don't want to overpay for the shares of other companies, and it would be value-destroying if we were to overpay when we are buying Berkshire.

Stockholders may well interpret share repurchases as a signal that the company believes that its stock is undervalued by Mr. Market. This signal may explain why repurchase announcements often give a stock's price a little bump.

Looking at the JBW equation, Gary needed values for dividends (plus repurchases) D, a required return R, and a dividend growth rate g:

$$JBW : V = \frac{D}{R - g}$$

Adjusting for the way the S&P 500 index is calculated, Gary estimated the annual dividends plus buybacks to be 194 in 2021. Considering the huge surge in repurchases shown in Fig. 2.9 for 2021, Gary used the conservative value $D = 150$. For a required return, the interest rates on Treasury bonds were 2.88% for 10-year bonds and 3.11% for 30-year bonds at the time. Gary used an 8% required return—which also seemed conservative—but he invited readers to make their own calculations.

The last input Gary needed was the future rate of growth of S&P 500 dividends plus repurchases. Since 1998, the annual growth rates had been about 6% for dividends and 10% for repurchases. For the sum, dividends plus buybacks, Gary used the seemingly conservative value of 5%, which is a little lower than the long-run growth of U.S. GDP.

With these cautious assumptions, Williams' valuation equation gave an intrinsic value of 5000:

$$V = \frac{\$150}{0.08 - 0.05} = 5000$$

which was 31% above the 3818.37 value of the S&P at that time.

Since the required rate of return varies from investor to investor, it is often helpful to calculate the intrinsic value for a wide range of values for

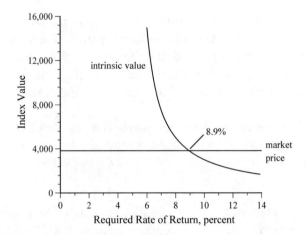

Fig. 2.10 The intrinsic value of the S&P 500 for different required rates of return

the required return, as is shown in Fig. 2.10. The breakeven required rate of return is 8.9%, which means that the estimated intrinsic value exceeds the market price for any required return below 8.9%. At the time, with Treasury bonds yielding around 3%, that seemed like a very attractive breakeven rate.

Gary concluded:

> Nobody knows where stock prices will be next week, next month, or at the end of the year. But a range of plausible, conservative assumptions about the future cash flow from stocks indicates that it is highly likely that the intrinsic value of the S&P 500 is currently above its market price. Stocks are cheap.

Gary's conclusion was not a prediction about future stock prices. It was his opinion that people who bought the S&P 500 stocks in July 2022 would be happy they did.

What About Risk?

In 2008 many investors were bearish on the car company Volkswagen. Some not only sold the shares they owned but also borrowed shares from other investors and sold these too. These *short-sellers* were hoping to buy Volkswagen stock at some future date at a low price so that they could replace the shares they had borrowed, with profits equal to the difference between the price at which they sold the borrowed shares and the price they paid to replace them. In October 2008, 480 million Volkswagen shares had been sold short, 12% of all Volkswagen stock.

Then the short-sellers were blindsided. On October 28, 2008, Porsche announced that they had bought 74% of Volkswagen's stock. The state of Lower Saxony owned another 20%. Neither had any intention of selling. That left 240 million shares that could be bought by short-sellers who needed to buy 480 million shares to replace the shares they had borrowed. This was the short-squeeze of all short-squeezes. The short-sellers were legally obligated to replace the stock they borrowed, no matter how much they had to pay to do it.

Volkswagen's stock price jumped 93 percent in a single day as short-sellers scrambled to cover their positions before they lost even more money. Then Porsche generously decided to sell some of its holdings as a lifebuoy for short-sellers (and to take advantage of the artificially high prices). The short-squeeze ended and Volkswagen's stock price fell back to its level before the squeeze.

Wild and crazy stories like these have persuaded many investors that the stock market is nothing more than legalized gambling—something that prudent people should avoid. Indeed, many people, including some of our friends and relatives, think the stock market is a white-collar scam where the insiders fleece the unwitting. They're wrong. Financial scams do exist, but the overall stock market is not one.

Still, it is a harsh reality that stock prices do not march steadily upward but are instead buffeted by news, rumors, fear, and greed. One glaring inadequacy of the Investing 2.0 paradigm is that it teaches us how to estimate what a stock is worth but not how to gauge the risks involved in stock investing—even though all investors know there are risks. The next giant development in investment strategies—what we call Investing 3.0—tackles the measurement of risk head-on.

References

Buffett, Warren. 2021. Berkshire Hathaway Shareholder Letter. https://www.berkshirehathaway.com/letters/2021ltr.pdf.
Denning, Tim. 2020. The Stock Market Is a Ponzi Scheme, *Medium*, July 3.
Graham, Benjamin. 1954. *The Intelligent Investor*, New York: Harper.
Graham, Benjamin, and Dodd, David L. 1934. *Security Analysis*, New York: McGraw-Hill.
Williams, John Burr. 1938. *The Theory of Investment Value*, Cambridge, MA: Harvard University Press.

3

Investing 3.0—(Mis)measuring Risk

John Burr Williams did not explicitly consider risk beyond the recommendation that an investor's personal interest rate should be somewhat higher than the interest rates on Treasury bonds. Benjamin Graham also treated risk loosely, simply advising investors to not pay more than a price that allows a margin of safety, "rendering unnecessary an accurate estimate of the future." Warren Buffett explained margin of safety with his usual clarity:

> You have to have the knowledge to enable you to make a very general estimate about the value of the underlying business. But you do not cut it close. That is what Ben Graham meant by having a margin of safety. You don't try to buy businesses worth $83 million for $80 million. You leave yourself an enormous margin. When you build a bridge, you insist it can carry 30,000 pounds, but you only drive 10,000 pound trucks across it. And that same principle works in investing.

Williams and Graham did not suggest a method for quantifying risk or for gauging how some combinations of stocks might be safer than other combinations. The Investing 3.0 revolution did just that.

Mean–Variance Analysis

In the 1950s Harry Markowitz and James Tobin noted that investor uncertainty about a stock's prospective return might be summarized by the bell-shaped normal distribution, which depends solely on the statistical mean and standard deviation of the distribution. For example, Fig. 3.1 shows a normal distribution for a stock's annual return that has a mean of 10% and a standard deviation of 20%. Some useful properties of normal distributions are that there is a 0.68 (roughly two-thirds) probability of a value within one standard deviation of the mean and a 0.95 probability of a value within two standard deviations. For the normal distribution in Fig. 3.1, there is a two-thirds probability that the return will be between −10% and +30%, and a 0.95 probability that the return will be between −30% and +50%.

It is natural to measure the riskiness of a stock by the standard deviation of its return—the higher the standard deviation, the less certain is the return.

Figure 3.2 compares the distribution in Fig. 3.1, which has a 10% mean and 20% standard deviation to a normal distribution that has a 5% mean and 10% standard deviation. The second distribution has a somewhat lower mean, but the smaller standard deviation implies that its return is less uncertain. The return on the second stock is far less likely, for example, to be below −20%, −30%, or −40%.

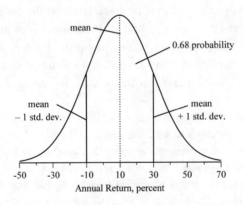

Fig. 3.1 A normal distribution with a 10% mean and 20% standard deviation

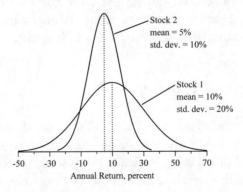

Fig. 3.2 Two normal distributions

This model of risk is known as *mean–variance analysis* (or *Modern Portfolio Theory*) although, as here, we often work with standard deviations which are equal to the square root of the variance.

The Markowitz Frontier

The value-investing approach of John Burr Williams and Ben Graham generally evaluates stocks and other investments individually. Is Apple attractively priced? What about Google? Johnson & Johnson? The main insights of mean–variance analysis, in contrast, come from considering how the stocks in an investor's portfolio fit together.

To illustrate, we used monthly data for the period 2003 through 2007 to estimate the means, standard deviations, and correlations for the returns on three stocks: AT&T, IBM, and Coke. We then used these estimates to determine the means and standard deviations for portfolios that are invested in various combinations of these three stocks. The three black circles in Fig. 3.3 are the means and standard deviations for the three individual stocks. By varying the amount of money invested in each stock, a portfolio can have any combination of risk and return that is inside the curved lines in Fig. 3.3. One of the main lessons of mean–variance analysis is that there are lots of portfolios that have lower standard deviations than any of the individual stocks. Here, many of the portfolios inside the curved lines in Fig. 3.3 have a lower standard deviation than AT&T, IBM, or Coke. Diversification pays!

The top of the curved-line region in Fig. 3.3 is darkened to show the maximum possible mean for each possible standard deviation. These optimal

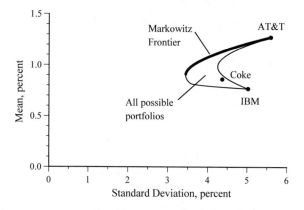

Fig. 3.3 The Markowitz Frontier

Table 3.1 Some Portfolios on the Markowitz Frontier

Mean, %	Standard Deviation, %	Portfolio allocation, %		
		AT&T	IBM	Coke
0.90	3.44	17	34	49
1.00	3.66	40	20	39
1.10	4.21	62	7	30
1.20	4.91	83	0	17
1.27	5.59	100	0	0

portfolios dominate all other portfolios and are called the *Markowitz frontier* in recognition of Harry Markowitz's pioneering work.

A book based on the Public Broadcasting System series *Beyond Wall Street* offered this description of a Markowitz frontier:

> *The curves illustrate maximum return at the various levels of risk that an investor is willing to assume. Investments above the curve have too much risk. Below the curve, the returns are too low. Goldilocks would say that the risk along the curve is not too hot and not too cold; it's just right.*

That's cute, but silly. The Markowitz frontier describes opportunities, not preferences, and it is not possible to go above the Markowitz frontier.

Some of the portfolios on the Markowitz frontier in Fig. 3.3 are listed in Table 3.1. Investors can choose among the portfolios on the Markowitz frontier based on their risk preferences. The seriously risk averse, for example, would invest heavily in Coke because this reduces the portfolio's standard deviation. Notice, though, that even the most risk averse find it advantageous to diversify their portfolios by including the riskiest stock, AT&T. The less risk averse hold less Coke and more AT&T. The least risk averse go all AT&T.

Tobin's Separation Theorem

Now let's introduce a safe asset like Treasury bills. If we are thinking about a one-year horizon for our investments, one-year Treasury bills are 100% safe because we know (or, at least, hope) that the federal government will not go bankrupt and we know exactly how much money we will receive at the end of one year. The standard deviation of our return on one-year Treasury bills is 0.

Figure 3.4 shows that the possibilities for combining a safe asset (like Treasury bills) with a risky asset (like a stock or stock portfolio) are given by a straight line between the two. A 50–50 investment is at the midpoint of the line. An increased investment in the risky asset moves up the line; more Treasury bills move down the line.

In our AT&T/IBM/Coke example, a safe asset, like Treasury bills, can be combined with any of the stock portfolios in Fig. 3.3. Figure 3.5 shows that when this is done, there is one optimal stock portfolio—where a straight line from the safe asset (Treasury bills) is tangent to the Markowitz frontier—because, for any level of risk, the highest possible mean is on this straight line.

Figure 3.5 uses a safe return of 0.24%, which was the average monthly return on T-bills during the period 2003 through 2007. The optimal stock

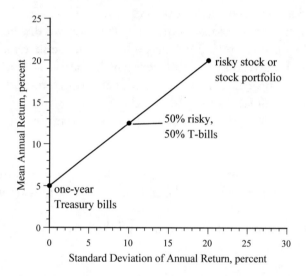

Fig. 3.4 Combining a safe investment with a risky investment

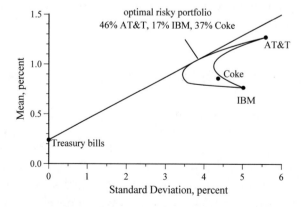

Fig. 3.5 The optimal risky portfolio

portfolio is 46% AT&T, 17% IBM, and 37% Coke. Even though Coke and IBM have much lower means than AT&T, they earn a place in the optimal portfolio because of their diversification value.

Each investment possibility shown by the straight line in Fig. 3.5 represents a combination of Treasury bills and this 46%-17%-37% optimal stock portfolio. The extremely risk averse might put all their money in Treasury bills. The less risk averse might put half their money in Treasury bills and half in the optimal stock portfolio, divided 46% AT&T, 17% IBM, and 37% Coke. The more venturesome might put all (or almost all) their money in the optimal stock portfolio, divided in the same proportions.

The 46%-17%-37% optimal combination of AT&T, IBM, and Coke in Fig. 3.5 does not depend on risk preferences. This is Tobin's *Separation Theorem*: investment decisions can be separated into two distinct parts: first, determine the optimal stock portfolio and, second, use investor preferences to determine the division of wealth between the safe asset and the optimal stock portfolio. This contradicts the traditional investment-advisory practice of selecting different stocks for different clients.

Mean–variance analysis is mathematically elegant and offers several valuable insights:

1. A diversified stock portfolio may be safer than any stock in the portfolio.
2. The gains from diversification depend on the correlations among the stock returns.
3. A combination of stocks and Treasury bills is safer than a portfolio of low-risk stocks.

Much of the early empirical work on diversified portfolios focused on U.S. stocks. However, portfolio risk can be reduced further by considering a wider range of assets; for example, real estate, natural resources, and foreign stocks and bonds. Diversification reduces risk.

Some Problems with Mean–Variance Analysis

Mean–variance analysis helped move investing strategies beyond Investing 2.0, which evaluated stocks in isolation, to a mathematical analysis of the riskiness of stock portfolios. This was an impressive intellectual accomplishment (which was rewarded with multiple Nobel Prizes). However, there are debilitating problems with using mean–variance analysis to gauge risk. The two primary problems are: (1) stocks returns are not normally distributed and

(2) past returns are not a reliable guide to the future. Even more damning, from our viewpoint, is that mean–variance analysis focuses on price volatility, which should be of little concern to most investors. Instead of reinforcing the value-investing argument that it is all about the income from stocks, mean–variance analysis makes it all about short-term price fluctuations.

Stock Returns Are Not Normally Distributed

Mean–variance analysis assumes that the only metrics that matter to investors are the mean and standard deviation of their portfolio returns. This would make sense if returns were normally distributed, but they are not.

Figure 3.6 compares the actual distribution of the monthly returns for the S&P 500 with a theoretical normal distribution. The distribution looks bell shaped—roughly symmetrical with the curve rising gradually and then rapidly to a peak—and 96% of the returns are within two standard deviations of the mean, compared to a theoretical 95%. However, one obvious disparity is the "high peak" in that there are more observations clustered close to the mean than is true of a normal distribution. If the returns were normally distributed, 68% of the returns would be within one standard deviation of the mean. Here, 76% are.

The most important discrepancy in Fig. 3.6, however, is arguably the "fat tails"—the extreme observations that are far from the mean. There are not a lot of them—just a few scattered returns below minus 20% and a few more above positive 20%—but these large outliers can be critically important. A

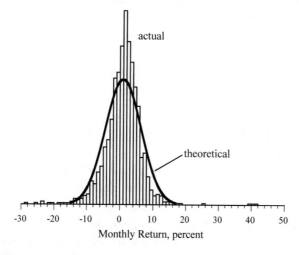

Fig. 3.6 S&P 500 monthly returns, 1926 through 2022

20% return in one month can be exhilarating; a 20% loss can be devastating. With a normal distribution using the historical mean and standard deviation of monthly returns, such large price swings are essentially impossible, yet they happened several times. A month as bad as September 1931, with a −28.7% return, should happen less than once in every 4 million years, and a month as good as April 1933, with a 41.4% return, should happen less than once in every 2 trillion years. Yet, they both happened in less than 100 years.

It is not just monthly returns. There have also been some spectacularly terrific and terrible individual days. On October 19, 1987, the S&P 500 return was negative 19.5% and, two days later, on October 21, 1987, it was positive 8.8%. On March 15, 1933, the S&P return was 16.8%. With a normal distribution, none of these should have happened in several trillion years.

This is called the *black swan problem*. The English used to believe that black swans did not exist because all the swans they had ever seen or read about were white. However, logically, no matter how many white swans we see, this can never prove that all swans are white. Sure enough, a Dutch explorer found black swans in Australia in 1697.

The fact that, up until October 19, 1987, the S&P 500 had never risen or fallen by more than 19% in a single day, did not prove that it could not happen. Unfortunately, it is nigh impossible to make accurate estimates of the chances of rare events because we observe them so rarely.

In August 2007, twenty years after the October 19, 1987, crash (and presumably taking that crash into account), Lehman Brothers' head of quantitative strategies told *The Wall Street Journal* that, "Events that models only predicted would happen once in 10,000 years happened every day for three days." Long-Term Capital Management was a hedge fund run by some of the brightest financial experts, but the risk models they constructed said that the losses that they incurred on one day in Augusta 1998 should have happened only once in 80 trillion years. Nonetheless, losses that catastrophic happened—and then happened again the next week.

The Past Is Not a Reliable Guide to the Future

For the illustrative mean–variance analysis shown in Figs. 3.4 and 3.5, we blithely used the 2003–2007 means, standard deviations, and correlations for the monthly returns on AT&T, IBM, and Coke as if we were confident that they applied to the future as well as the past. Were you skeptical? You should have been. It is dangerous to use historical data to estimate future opportunities. Yet, that is what almost all mean–variance practitioners do.

During the five-year period 2003 through 2007, AT&T stock happened to do much better than IBM or Coke, but it would be foolish to assume that AT&T will always outperform IBM and Coke. These are all well-known companies, followed closely by well-compensated analysts. Most investors were surely surprised by AT&T's superior performance during the years 2003 through 2007 and were certainly not confident of a repeat performance during the next five years.

Table 3.2 shows that AT&T's average monthly return over the next five years, 2008 through 2012, went from first to worst.

This loose relationship between past and future returns is not unusual. Figure 3.7 shows the relationship between the 2003–2007 average returns and the 2008–2012 average returns for all 30 stocks in the Dow Jones Industrial Average. The correlation is slightly negative, −0.10, but so close to zero as to be meaningless.

Even more unreasonable than the assumption that superior stock performance will persist is the assumption that terrible stock performance is permanent. For example, Pfizer had a negative return during the period 2003–2007 but investors who held Pfizer at the beginning of 2008 surely did

Table 3.2 Mean monthly returns, 2003–2007 and 2008–2012

	Mean Return (%)	
	2003–2007	2008–2012
AT&T	1.273	0.284
IBM	0.768	1.267
Coke	0.860	0.655

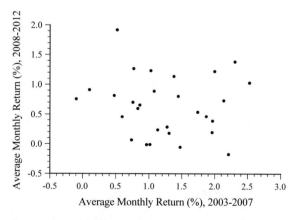

Fig. 3.7 Correlation between average monthly returns in 2003–2007 and 2008–2012

not anticipate a negative return over the next five years, so it would have been foolish to do a mean–variance analysis using a negative expected return for Pfizer. As it turned out, Pfizer had a positive return during the next five years. This was not an isolated case. During the 5-year period 2008 through 2012, four companies (Cisco, General Electric, Goldman Sachs, and Microsoft) had negative average returns. We should not do mean–variance analysis assuming negative expected returns unless we have a good reason for doing so. The fact that there happened to be negative returns is the past is not a good reason.

Historical standard deviations are not much more reliable than historical average returns. Figure 3.8 is a scatter diagram of the monthly 2003–2007 standard deviations and 2008–2012 standard deviations for the 30 Dow stocks. The correlation is a modest 0.26. Similarly, Fig. 3.9 compares the 2003–2007 and 2008–2012 correlations between the returns for the Dow stocks. The correlation among these correlations is an unreliable 0.30. Not only is there not a close correlation, but many values are implausibly large or small, even negative.

Mean–variance analysis is supposed to help investors choose a portfolio for the future and it consequently requires values for the future means, standard deviations, and correlations. It is perilous to use past values because there is typically little relationship between the past and future values of the means, standard deviations, and correlations.

The conclusion is indisputable. Choosing an investment portfolio based on past returns is foolhardy. To make this argument more concrete, Fig. 3.10 shows what happens when we add Pfizer and McDonald's to our AT&T, IBM, and Coke portfolio using data from 2003 through 2007. The optimal

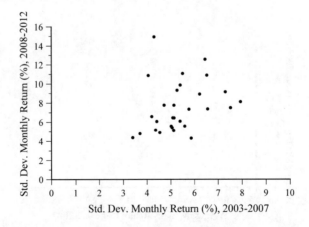

Fig. 3.8 Correlation between standard deviations of monthly returns

3 Investing 3.0—(Mis)measuring Risk

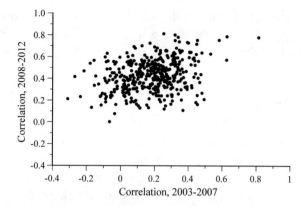

Fig. 3.9 Relationship between correlations of monthly returns

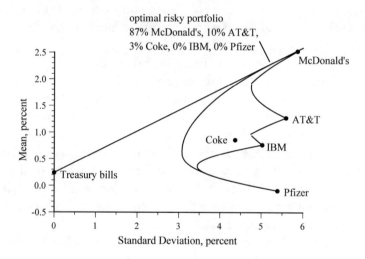

Fig. 3.10 Historical returns can lead to unbalanced portfolios

risky portfolio is 87% McDonald's, 10% AT&T, 3% Coke, 0% IBM, and 0% Pfizer. Mean–variance analysis preaches the value of diversification, but mean–variance analysis based on historical data is likely to favor highly unbalanced portfolios, invested heavily in stocks that have done well in the past and ignoring stocks that have done poorly.

Most practitioners know this and, so, they impose limits; for example, no more than 10% of a portfolio can be invested in any single stock. This rule keeps implausible estimates of the means, standard deviations, and correlations from creating unbalanced portfolios, but it is also an admission that the estimates are implausible. These limits are just a clumsy hack to cover up the consequences of bad assumptions. It would be much better to make plausible assumptions that reflect an investor's beliefs. Then the selected portfolio will reflect those beliefs, too.

The Yale Model

We have seen that historical data can lead to unbalanced portfolios that are heavily invested in those stocks that happened to have high means, low standard deviations and low correlations with other stock returns, the opposite of the diversification recommended by mean–variance analysis.

We also noted that some investors deal with this problem by tweaking the outputs so that no single investment can be more than a preset fraction of its portfolio. It is better to tweak the inputs, and some do. Perhaps the most famous example is David Swensen, who managed Yale's endowment portfolio from 1985 until his death in 2021.

A time-honored tradition in the heartland is for farmers to gather for morning coffee and to fret about the weather and farm prices. David Swensen grew up in River Falls, Wisconsin, population 5000, listening to radio reports of corn prices rising and falling. He later said that he was fascinated with "the idea that every day these prices would change. What caused that?".

Swensen went to college at the University of Wisconsin—River Falls, where his father was a chemistry professor. His mother became a Lutheran minister after her six children had grown up. Swensen enrolled in Yale's graduate economics program in 1975, an enthusiastic Midwesterner who sometimes wore bib overalls to class.

At Yale, his Ph.D. thesis developed a model for explaining changes in corporate bond prices. He got the data he needed from Salomon Brothers and they were so impressed that they hired him when he finished his thesis in 1979. After three years in their bond department, Swensen moved to Lehman Brothers to handle swaps, a novel financial instrument that he had originated at Salomon.

Meanwhile, back at Yale, the inflation-adjusted value of Yale's endowment had fallen by nearly half between 1968 and 1979. One of Swensen's thesis advisors, William Brainard, was now provost and wanted to hire Swensen to manage Yale's portfolio. It was an unconventional choice for Yale, since Swensen had never been a portfolio manager, and an unconventional idea for Swensen, since he would have to take an 80% pay cut.

The job was offered and Swensen took it in 1985, later admitting that "I'm not quite sure why it is they would have chosen me," and explaining that he accepted because, "There are a lot of important things in life you don't measure in dollars and cents." For Swensen, some of these things were teaching college students, playing poker with James Tobin (another of Swensen's thesis advisers), watching Yale hockey games, and coaching his children's baseball and soccer teams.

It all worked out. A 2005 cover story for the *Yale Alumni Magazine* was titled, "Yale's $8 billion man," referring to the fact that Yale $14 billion endowment would have would have been $8 billion lower if it had had the same investment returns as the average college and university endowment over the preceding twenty years. In 2021, Yale reported that Swensen's value added over the preceding thirty years, taking into account Yale's spending out of the endowment, was $47 billion.

How did Swensen do it? Mean–variance analysis. When Swensen came to Yale in 1985 to manage the endowment portfolio, he talked with Brainard and Tobin and decided that, if we really believe this stuff, let's use it. In a 2018 reunion speech Swensen said, with his usual boyish enthusiasm, "For a given level of return, if you diversify you can get that return at lower risk. For a given level of risk, if you diversify you can get a higher return. That's pretty cool! Free lunch!".

Instead of selecting individual stocks, Swensen looked at the eight asset classes shown in Table 3.3. U. S. cash, bonds, and stocks are just what they seem and, at the time, were the mainstays of college endowment portfolios. Many colleges followed the 60/40 rule: 60% stocks, 40% bonds. Yale wasn't much different when Swensen took over in 1985.

Table 3.3 shows how Swensen drastically reduced Yale's investment in U.S. stocks and diversified into nontraditional asset classes. A new asset class for Yale (and all educational institutions) was what Swensen called *absolute return* strategies that try to exploit market inefficiencies and special situations like mergers, spinoffs, and bankruptcies. These investments are hedged

Table 3.3 The changes that Swensen wrought, percent of Yale endowment

	1985	2000
Cash	10	8
U.S. bonds	10	9
U.S. stocks	62	14
Developed stocks	6	5
Emerging stocks	0	5
Absolute return	0	20
Real Estate	9	15
Private equity	3	24

so that the payoff doesn't depend on a market going up or down, only that the inefficiency or special situation works out okay. Other people call these market-neutral strategies. Swensen also upped Yale's investment in real estate and he made private equity the largest component of Yale's portfolio. Private equity includes venture capital and leveraged buyouts and has been Yale's most profitable asset class.

The implementation of the details of Yale's portfolio strategy is left to a hundred or so outside managers and specialists in the various asset classes.

How did Swensen get from the 1985 portfolio to the 2000 portfolio? Mean–variance analysis requires means, standard deviations, and correlations for the eight asset classes. Swensen quickly recognized that historical values might not only be unrealistic predictions of the future but also lead to severely unbalanced portfolios.

Swensen figured that the historical means were the most likely to be misleading and dangerous. If, for example, emerging stocks had happened to do extraordinarily well during the historical period he looked at, it would be foolish to assume that emerging stocks would continue to do extraordinarily well in the future and be lured into building a portfolio that was, say, 90% invested in emerging stocks. So, he adjusted the historical means to reflect realistic future expectations.

Another of Swensen's core principle was to trust markets to price assets to give reasonable expected returns. Specifically, he assumed that similar assets are priced to have similar expected returns and dissimilar assets are priced to have different expected returns.

Swensen worked with real, inflation-adjusted returns. Table 3.4 shows the historical means and the adjusted values he used as inputs for his mean–variance analysis in 2000.

Historically, the average inflation-adjusted return on cash (Treasury bills and other short-term investments) had been slightly negative, but Swensen

Table 3.4 Inflation-adjusted means, percent

	Historical data	2000 adjusted values
Cash	−0.4	0.0
U.S. bonds	1.2	2.0
U.S. stocks	9.2	6.0
Developed stocks	6.3	6.0
Emerging stocks	11.1	8.0
Absolute return	17.6	7.0
Real estate	3.5	4.0
Private equity	19.1	12.5

figured that a zero percent real return was more reasonable. Swensen also felt that the historical eight percentage-point difference between the average returns on U.S. stocks and bonds was unreasonably large, as was the historical three percentage-point difference between the average returns on U.S. stocks and stocks in other developed countries. Perhaps the U.S. stock market had simply done better in the past than investors had anticipated? Whatever the reason, Swensen assumed that, going forward, the expected return on U.S. stocks should be comparable to that for other developed countries and that the risk premium over U.S. bonds should be four percentage points. So, he set the mean return on U.S. bonds at two percent and the mean returns on stocks in the United States and in other developed countries at 6%.

Stocks in emerging countries are riskier because their economies are more fragile and there are substantial political risks, so Swensen reasoned that investors would price them to have somewhat higher expected returns. He assumed 8%.

Real estate is a hybrid of bonds and stocks because long-term leases provide a steady income (like bonds), while real estate prices increase over time (like stocks). He put the expected return at 4%, halfway between U.S. bonds and stocks. The historical returns on absolute return and private equity investments have been spectacular but are overstated by the exclusion of investments that failed, so he reduced their means substantially.

For a few years, Swensen did Yale's mean–variance analysis using the adjusted means together with the historical standard deviations and correlations. Then he adjusted the standard deviations. For example, the historical standard deviation of U.S. bond returns had been dampened by long periods in which interest rates hardly changed at all. Swensen anticipated that there would be more interest rate volatility in the future than in the past and adjusted the standard deviation upward. The biggest adjustment was to real estate. The historical standard deviation was lower than for any other asset class (except cash). Surely, this is misleading. Most commercial real estate is held for a long time; so we only see the price when it is bought and the price when it is sold decades later. We don't see the annual fluctuations in market value along the way. Because real estate is a hybrid of bonds and stocks, Swensen assumed a standard deviation halfway between the two.

After a few years of using adjusted means and standard deviations, Swensen tackled the correlation coefficients. The historical data had several negative correlations, but he figured that these were coincidental and that there was no logical reason to expect any of the returns to be negatively correlated in the future. So, he assumed more reasonable values going forward. He also tweaked several positive historical correlations.

The use of mean–variance analysis together with these adjusted means, standard deviations, and correlations led to the 2000 portfolio allocation shown in Table 3.3.

Swensen didn't change the adjusted means, standard deviations, and correlations much from year to year, so the portfolio allocation didn't change much either. One consequence of holding the target portfolio allocation constant is that it forces an automatic portfolio rebalancing when one asset class does much better or worse than others. If emerging stocks did spectacularly well, Swensen sold some to get back to the target portfolio allocation. If the U.S. stock market crashes, Swensen bought stocks to get back to the target level. This rebalancing is an automatic contrarian strategy. Sell what has gone up, buy what has gone down.

Over time, Yale's asset classes have been modified a bit and so have the means, standard deviations, and correlations. Table 3.5 shows that the 2021 Yale portfolio had eight broad asset classes. Developed and emerging stocks were combined into one category (foreign stocks) and so were cash and U.S. bonds. The real estate position went down a bit, while natural resources were added. Yale doesn't buy stock in companies that own oil, gas, and timber. Yale buys oil fields, gas fields, and forests. Leveraged buyouts were now a separate category with a substantial investment.

The most striking feature of the 2021 Yale portfolio is that U.S. cash, bonds, and stocks have been reduced to 10% (compared to 82% in 1985). The effective disappearance of U.S. stocks from Yale's portfolio was, in retrospect, a mistake. For the fiscal year ending on June 30, 2022, the Yale endowment's annual return was a respectable 12.0% over the previous ten years, well above the average college endowment, but the S&P 500 return was a percentage point higher, at 13.0%.

Beyond the mathematics of mean–variance analysis, there were two secrets to Swensen's success. One was his abandonment of the 60/40 rule used by most college endowment managers. The intent of this popular guideline is

Table 3.5 The 2021 Yale Portfolio, percent of Yale endowment

U.S. cash and bonds	8
U.S. stocks	2
Foreign stocks	12
Absolute return	23
Real Estate	10
Natural resources	5
Venture capital	23
Leveraged buyouts	17

to use a heavy investment on bonds to dampen short-term fluctuations in endowment values; the consequence has been to dampen long-run returns. Swensen's discarding of the 60/40 rule made Yale look great relative to other college endowments.

The second secret was the substantial investment in nontraditional asset classes—not because they are inherently better than stocks and bonds but because there is much more variation in the abilities of nontraditional asset managers, and Swensen was extraordinarily successful in identifying superior managers. It has been estimated that some 50–80% of Yale's success in outperforming other colleges and universities was due to Swensen's knack for finding managers who outperform the average manager in their asset class.

What explains Swensen's success in identifying superior managers? Gary was on Swensen's thesis committee (along with Tobin and Brainard) and believes that a lot of Swensen's success came from his clear-headed midwestern upbringing. Oddly enough, when Gary thinks of Swensen, he thinks of Pauline Esther Friedman and her identical twin sister, Esther Pauline Friedman, two Iowa women who wrote the wildly popular advice columns Dear Abby and Ask Ann Landers for some fifty years. They were known for being compassionate, wise, witty, and (above all) sensible. Here is one example from Dear Abby:

The best index to a person's character is how he treats people who can't do him any good, and how he treats people who can't fight back.

One more. A reader once asked for advice about some people he didn't care for who had moved into the neighborhood: "Abby, these weirdos are wrecking our property values! How can we improve the quality of this once-respectable neighborhood?" Abby's answer was simple and to the point: "You could move."

In the same way, Swensen's approach was straightforward, sensible, and to the point: think about what a person is saying and think about the person saying it. In a 2009 interview, Swensen stressed the importance of dealing with people you trust: "The most important thing is character and the quality of people. That's also the second most important thing and the third most important thing. It's everything." Swensen's character assessment was based on his read of the person and interviews with people who had known the prospective manager in a wide variety of contexts, in some cases going all the way back to high school teachers.

It seems corny, but it worked. Swensen turned down one manager who later crashed and burned because the only thing Swensen knew for certain about his strategy was that he was greedy. Talking about Bernie Madoff, who turned out to be running a massive Ponzi scheme, Swensen said, "If you sat down and had a conversation with him about his investment activities and couldn't figure out that he was being evasive, shame on you."

A Myopic Focus on Short-Term Volatility

Fat tails and misleading historical data can make mean–variance analysis treacherous. An even more insidious problem is that it abandons value investing. A value investor focuses on the anticipated future income from an investment. The primary risk is that the future income may turn out to be substantially below what was expected. Mean–variance analysis, in contrast, measures risk by the volatility of short-term returns—which is primarily caused by short-run fluctuations in market prices.

An obsession with short-run price volatility is the reason that many investment advisors recommend bond-heavy portfolio allocations like these:

> 50% stocks, 50% bonds
> 60% stocks, 40% bonds
> 40% stocks, 40% bonds, 20% cash.

Stocks have outperformed bonds by substantial margins historically and often offer more attractive potential returns going forward. Nonetheless, many people make the mistake of investing unreasonable amounts in bonds and cash in order to dampen short-term fluctuations in the market value of their portfolio.

For investors who do not depend on selling stock to pay their living expenses, short-run price volatility should be of little concern. If anything, fluctuations in market prices can be beneficial because they may offer opportunities for buying or selling at favorable prices. If Mr. Market's prices are unreasonably high or low, value investors can take advantage of Mr. Market's foolishness. As Warren Buffett wrote,

> *To refer to a personal taste of mine, I'm going to buy hamburgers the rest of my life. When hamburgers go down in price, we sing the 'Hallelujah Chorus' in the Buffett household. When hamburgers go up in price, we weep. For most people, it's the same with everything in life they will be buying — except stocks. When stocks go down and you can get more for your money, people don't like them anymore.*

Deferring Gains and Harvesting Losses

Fluctuating stock prices also have important tax consequences that can boost investment returns. If the market prices of some of your stocks have gone up, these capital gains are taxable; but you don't pay the taxes until you realize the gains by selling the stocks. If, for instance, you buy 1000 shares of a stock for $20 a share and the price rises to $30, you have a $10,000 capital gain but you don't have to pay a tax on this gain unless you sell the stock. If it is a short-term gain (held for a year or less) it is generally taxed as ordinary income; if it is a long-term gain (held for more than a year), it is taxed at a lower rate (typically 15%). Either way, realizing the gain and paying a tax leaves you with less money to invest. If you don't sell, the government has effectively loaned you your tax liability, and the only "interest" you pay on this loan is taxes on the extra dividends and capital gains. Even better, there is no capital gains tax at all if the stock is held until your death since your heirs do not pay taxes on capital gains that occurred before they receive their inheritance. No bank will loan you money at such favorable terms.

The lower tax rate on long-term gains provides an obvious incentive to defer the realization of gains, at least until they become lightly taxed long-term gains. Even after a year, there are persistent benefits from postponing taxes in order to continue earning dividends and capital gains on the deferred taxes.

Table 3.6 shows some illustrative calculations for a portfolio that is initially worth $100,000. Every year for 30 years, the portfolio earns 5% dividends and 5% capital gains, a total return of 10%. The buy-and-hold strategy is to never sell so that the only taxes paid are a 15% tax on the dividends. The "annual trader" strategy is to turn the portfolio over every year, holding each year's portfolio just long enough to qualify for a 15% long-term capital gains tax rate. The "active trader" strategy is to never hold a stock for more than a year, so capital gains are taxed at a 24% rate.

Turnover deflates performance dramatically, illustrating the old saying, "The broker made money, the IRS made money, and two out of three ain't bad!".

Table 3.6 Wealth for buy-and-hold vs. portfolio turnover

	10 years	20 years	30 years
Buy and Hold	$242,222	$586,717	$1,421,161
Annual Trader	$226,098	$511,205	$1,155,825
Active Trader	$216,894	$470,430	$1,020,336

On the other hand, it can be beneficial to sell stocks that have gone down in price because up to $3000 ($1500 if married, filing separately) of realized losses can be used to reduce taxable income. You can't make money by losing money; but once a loss has occurred, it can be profitable to realize the loss so that the tax credit can be invested. Suppose that the value of the 1000 shares you bought for $20,000 falls to $15,000. If you realize your $5000 loss by selling, you can deduct $3000 from your current taxable income and carry forward $2000 to be deducted from future income. In a 24% bracket, your $3000 loss reduces your taxes by $720, which you can invest. Instead of having $15,000 invested, you will have $15,720 earning dividends and (you hope) capital gains.

Some sophisticated investors deliberately choose a portfolio of volatile stocks in order to reap the tax benefits of deferring gains and harvesting losses. Instead of fearing price volatility, they embrace it! They hold on to those stocks that have appreciated (deferring gains) and sell those stocks that have done poorly (harvesting losses), reinvesting the proceeds in volatile stocks. We have investigated such strategies using a variety of plausible assumptions and found that a strategy of deferring gains and harvesting losses can increase wealth over long horizons by 10 to 40% relative to buy- and hold.

Untenable Independence

The mean–variance focus on price volatility might be rationalized by the questionable argument that the stock market is like a gambling casino in which stock prices fluctuate randomly, unrelated to long-run trends in corporate dividends and earnings.

Nobel Laureate Paul Samuelson offered this simple analogy. Find 150 years of monthly stock market returns and

> *Write down those 1,800 percentage changes in monthly stock prices on as many slips of paper. Put them in a big hat. Shake vigorously. Then draw at random a new couple of thousand tickets, each time replacing the last draw and shaking vigorously. That way we can generate new realistically representative possible histories of future equity markets.*

By Samuelson's reasoning, just like an unlucky gambler who might lose everything with a string of unfortunate wagers, so an unlucky investor might lose all of his or her money through several bad years in the stock market.

The problem with this argument is that long-run movements in stock prices are not simply the cumulation of independent draws of slips of paper from a hat but are, instead, anchored by corporate dividends and earnings. You can lose all your money betting on dice rolls because these are independent events. However, the S&P 500 will not go to zero. Stock prices will eventually stabilize and rebound because stocks will become temptingly cheap if earnings and dividends increase over time and stock prices don't. For similar reasons, stock market bubbles do not last forever.

The unwarranted assumption that investing in stocks is like rolling dice, drawing cards, or spinning a roulette wheel has led to some misleading conclusions and extraordinarily conservative advice. For example, Zvi Bodie, a prominent economist and financial advisor, once argued that,

> *Historically, stocks' standard deviation has been 20%. That means you shouldn't be at all surprised if you lose 16% rather than gain 4% in a given year. If you start out with $100,000 and lose 16%, you'll have $84,000 at the end of the first year. Then, if you lose another 16%, you'll have only $70,560 left, and so on.*

The unbounded "and so on" assumption is implausible (unless the economy also collapses by 16% every year). At some point, stock prices will be so low relative to corporate earnings and dividends that investors will find stocks irresistible and stock prices will stop free falling.

After the 2007–2008 stock crash, Bodie was even more apocalyptic:

> *Prices dropped by 37% last year. While improbable, there's nothing to say they couldn't drop by that much again next year or the year before you retire. And diversification doesn't take away that risk. That's why retirement money belongs in truly safe assets whose value won't go down—not in stocks.*

Instead of considering the 37% price drop a buying opportunity, Bodie feared that it might be just the first of many such declines. We disagree. A 37% price drop might be drawn over and over in a Samuelson simulation but won't happen in the real world.

In response to the question, "So should no one invest in stocks—not even the very wealthy?," Bodie responded as if 100% losses were a realistic possible outcome: "You should only invest in equities what you can afford to lose." How could anyone, especially a seasoned financial advisor, think that the S&P 500 could go to zero? Only by making the mathematically convenient but utterly unrealistic assumption that stock prices are like dice rolls.

With exquisitely bad timing, in March of 2009, Bodie advised people to sell all their stocks:

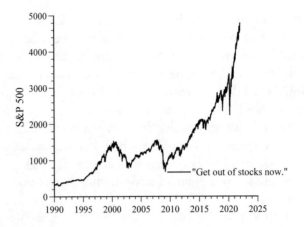

Fig. 3.11 Really, really bad timing

Unless you have the heart of a high stakes gambler, get out of stocks now and put your retirement money in inflation protected government bonds and similar instruments. These investments are immune to the kind of calamity Wall Street experienced last year.

In June 2009 an interviewer asked Bodie, "Wouldn't leaving the stock market right now be locking in your losses?" Bodie replied, with no evident irony, "That is exactly right. You want to make sure you don't lose more."

Figure 3.11 shows that the stock market bottomed on March 9, 2009, and then surged upward.

The point is not that Bodie was spectacularly wrong (we've all made mistakes), but that it is financially dangerous to think of the stock market as a gambling casino unhinged from the intrinsic value of stocks.

Stock Returns Are Not Random

Let's look more closely at the idea that stock returns can be modeled as random draws from either a big hat or a normal distribution. We looked at the monthly returns for the S&P 500 back to 1926, as far back as we have data. For each possible starting point in these historical data, we calculated the annual rate of return over horizons ranging from 5 to 50 years. Figure 3.12 shows the annual returns for the best, worst, and average starting months for each of these horizons.

For example, looking at the outcomes over all possible 50-year horizons, the very worst starting point was September 1929, right before the Great Crash. The annualized return over the next 50 years was 7.17%. At the other

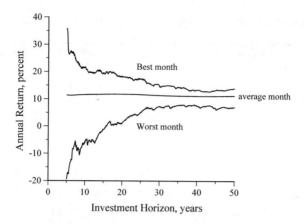

Fig. 3.12 Annual returns for best, worst, and average starting months

end of the worst-to-best spectrum, the very best starting point was July of 1949, with a 13.96% annual return over the next 50 years. The average annual return over all possible starting points was 11.25%.

It is particularly striking how profitable the stock market has been in the long run, even for the worst possible starting months. Notice, too, how the starting month becomes less important to the annual return as the horizon lengthens.

An important part of the reason that stocks have been a reliably profitable investment over long horizons is that stock returns are not random draws of paper from a hat or numbers from a probability distribution. Stock prices are ultimately tied to intrinsic values. As the nation's economy, corporate profits, and stock dividends grow over time, stock prices will ultimately increase too. Market prices may wander about, seemingly at random in the short run, but they are tethered to intrinsic values in the long run.

We also compared the historical returns to these two models that we have criticized:

Hat: This is the model described by Paul Samuelson. Monthly returns are drawn from a collection of all past monthly returns.

Normal: This is the model described by Zvi Bodie. Monthly returns are drawn from a normal distribution with a mean and standard deviation equal to the historical values.

Table 3.7 shows how often the Hat and Normal models generated wealth changes that were more extreme than anything ever experienced in the historical data. For example, over 50-year horizons, 10.04% of the wealth values

Table 3.7 Frequency with which wealth violated historical minimums or maximums, percent

	1-Month Horizon		25-year Horizon		50-Year Horizon	
	<Min	>Max	<Min	>Max	<Min	>Max
Hat	0.00	0.00	2.68	6.51	3.57	5.79
Normal	0.00	0.00	4.43	9.74	10.04	13.80

generated by the normal-distribution model that is consistent with mean–variance analysis and is so popular with finance professors were worse than had ever been experienced in any starting month in the historical data; 13.80% were better than had ever been experienced. Together, nearly a quarter of the wealth projections were more extreme than the most extreme numbers in the data.

The core problem is that long-run stock returns are not just the cumulation of a sequence of independent short-term price fluctuations. Models based on that assumption imply implausible results and should not be the basis for investment decisions. Nor are short-term price fluctuations the most appropriate measure of risk. In Chapter 6, we will show you a better way.

Yes, You Can Be Too Conservative

Earlier in this chapter we noted that many investment advisors try to reduce the short-term volatility of their clients' portfolios by recommending substantial bond holdings. One of the most popular strategies is a 60/40 portfolio (60% stocks, 40% bonds) based on the idea that a 60% investment in stocks will yield capital gains while a 40% investment in bonds reduces risk.

Our view is that short-term price volatility is relatively unimportant for investors with long horizons and that bonds can be a heavy drag on portfolio returns. For example, in December 2021, Gary did a financial analysis for a divorce case. Each spouse (we will call them Casey and Charlie) received an equal settlement of several million dollars in January 2013, with no child support or spousal support. Nine years later, Casey went back to court asking for spousal support because Charlie had started a successful business and the original settlement was not sufficient to maintain Casey's lifestyle.

Gary was asked to estimate a realistic return Casey might have earned on the settlement over this nine-year period and might earn in the future. One consideration was how Casey divided the investment between stocks and bonds. Gary assumed that the stocks would be an S&P 500 index fund and the bonds would be 10-year Treasury bonds. He considered three possible portfolios:

> 100% stocks
> 100% bonds
> 60/40 stocks/bonds

Figure 3.13 shows that the all-stock portfolio ran away with the race. Stocks had more short-run volatility, but their long-run return trounced the other strategies. This should not have been a surprise. In January 2013, when the divorce was finalized, the interest rate on 10-year Treasury bonds was 1.91%. The stocks in the S&P 500 had an average dividend yield of 2.20%. Not only was the dividend yield higher than the interest rate, but dividends and stock prices were likely to grow with the economy. In fact, the economy grew by about 50% during these 9 years and corporate earnings and dividends both more than doubled. Stock prices increased and, taking into account the substantial dividends, a dollar invested in the S&P 500 would have quadrupled.

Casey did not share in the bounty. In fact, Casey was even more conservative than a 60/40 or all-bonds strategy. Casey had put the entire divorce settlement into a checking account paying no interest at all—because Casey believed that stocks and bonds were "too risky." That's what comes of thinking that risk is gauged by short-term price swings.

A checking account paying no interest certainly minimizes short-term volatility, but at an enormous cost! After nine years, Casey's spending had reduced the bank balance by almost a third and Casey was rightly concerned

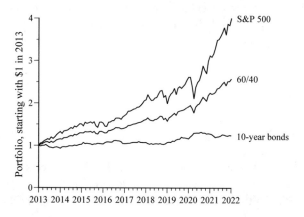

Fig. 3.13 Safe and sorry

that it would hit zero in the not-too-distant future—especially since the cost of living was increasing every year.

The judge in this case characterized Casey's investment approach as "extremely foolish" and noted that Casey's spending needs could easily be met "merely by adopting a more rational investment approach."

A Return to Investing 1.0

Mean–variance analysis provides many useful insights for investors, including the value of diversification, the importance of correlations among asset returns, and Tobin's separation theorem. However, the focus on short-term returns is of limited use and potentially misleading for investors with long horizons.

Instead of helping value investors deal with risk, mean–variance analysis brings us back into the Investing 1.0 morass of obsessing about short-term swings in stock prices. True value investors do not try to predict short-run returns and are not anxious about the possibility that stock prices might dip 5, 10, or even 30%. In fact, a fall in stock prices may be good news if it is not due to a drop in intrinsic values. A market panic can be a buying opportunity for value investors.

Warren Buffett once quipped that he and Charlie Munger should endow a chair to advance the teaching of modern portfolio theory because it gives them opportunities to buy great businesses at discounts to fair value.

In Chapter 6, we will introduce a better way to measure risk. Before we do that, we need to discuss the efficient market hypothesis, which contains some important insights but has also had the unfortunate consequence of diverting investor attention even further away from the timeless lessons of value investing and, instead, like modern portfolio theory, fixates on short-term price fluctuations.

References

Blackman, Stacy. 2009. Saving for retirement? MIT Sloan Prof Says "Sell Your Stocks", *MoneyWatch*, March 31.

Brandon, Emily. 2009. Stay safe, sell stocks: Zvi Bodie says retirees should go into conservative overdrive, *U.S. News & World Report*, June 13.

Bodie, Zvi. 1995. On the risk of stocks in the long run, *Financial Analysts Journal*, 51 (3), 18–22.

Buffett, Warren. 1984. The superinvestors of Graham-and-Doddsville, *Hermes, The Columbia Business School Magazine*, Fall, 4–15.
Buffett, Warren, and Loomis, Carol. 2001. Warren buffett on the stock market, *Fortune*, December.
BW Online. July 27, 2003. Online extra: sleep soundly without stocks. https://www.bloomberg.com/news/articles/2003-07-27/online-extra-sleep-soundly-without-stocks.
Chincarini, Ludwig. 2012. *The Crisis of Crowding: Quant Copycats, Ugly Models, and the New Crash Normal*, Bloomberg Press.
Constantinides, G. M. 1983. Capital market equilibrium with personal tax, *Econometrica*, 51, 611–636.
Constantinides, G. M. 1984. Optimal stock trading with personal taxes: implication for prices and the abnormal January return, *Journal of Financial Economics*, 13, 65–89.
Lakonishok, J., Shliefer, A., and Vishnu, R.W. 1994. Contrarian investment, extrapolation, and risk, *Journal of Finance*, 49, 1541–1578.
Light, Joe. 2009. You can't handle the truth about stocks, *CNN Money*, September 16.
Lowenstein, Roger. 2000. *When Genius Failed: The Rise and Fall of Long-term Capital Management*, New York: Random House.
Markowitz, Harry. 1959. *Portfolio Selection: Efficient Diversification of Investments*, New York: John Wiley & Sons.
Porterba, James M., and Summers, Lawrence H. 1988. Mean reversion in stock returns: Evidence and implications, *Journal of Financial Economics*, 22(1), 27–59.
Samuelson, Paul A. 1969. Lifetime portfolio selection by dynamic stochastic programming, *Review of Economics and Statistics*, 51(3), 239–246.
Samuelson, Paul A. 1997. Dogma of the day: Invest for the long term, the theory goes, and the risk lessens, *Bloomberg Personal Finance Magazine*, January/February.
Smith, Gary. 2016. Companies are seldom as good or as bad as they seem at the time, in *Toward a Just Society: Joseph Stiglitz and Twenty-First Century Economics*, M. Guzman, ed., 95–110. Columbia University Press.
Smith, Gary, and Xu, Albert. 2017. Stocks should be valued with a term structure of required returns, *Journal of Investing*, 26(2), 61–68.
Smith, Margaret Hwang, and Smith, Gary. 2008. Harvesting capital gains and losses, *Financial Services Review*, 17(4), 309–321.
Swensen, David F. 2000. *Pioneering Portfolio Management: An Unconventional Approach to Institutional Investment*, Free Press.
Swensen, David F. 2005. *Unconventional Success: A Fundamental Approach to Personal Investment*, New York: Free Press.
Tobin, James. 1958. Liquidity preference as behavior towards risk, *The Review of Economic Studies*, 25(2), 65–86.
Tobin, James. 1965. The theory of portfolio selection, in *The Theory of Interest Rates*, F. H. Hahn and F. P. R., eds. Brechling. London: Macmillan.

4

Investing 4.0—Efficient Markets and Value-Agnostic Indexing

Shortly after the appearance of mean–variance analysis in the 1950s, the efficient market hypothesis became popular in the 1960s. The theory is that stock prices take into account all relevant information so that no investor can beat the market by buying or selling stocks because they know something that other investors don't know.

Figure 4.1 shows a stylized example of an efficient market. This hypothetical stock's price wanders randomly until Day 10, jumps by $10 immediately after a positive news announcement, and then wanders randomly again. This stock's price jumps too fast for investors to make profits by buying the stock after the news announcement.

Important company announcements often happen after the stock market is closed, giving investors plenty of time to digest the news. When the market opens on the next trading day, the opening price reflects the impact of the news. In the Oracle example discussed in Chapter 2, the closing price for the final Oracle trade on Monday, December 8, 1997, was $32.375. Oracle announced its disappointing earnings after the Monday close and, when trading began the next day, the opening trade was at $23. Investors who held Oracle at the close of trading Monday were disappointed by the Monday news but they couldn't sell at Monday prices.

The Apple example we discussed in Chapter 2 was similar. Apple announced its quarterly results after the stock market closed on Wednesday, January 23, 2013. Apple's closing price that day was $514; the opening price on Thursday was $460. Investors could not sell *after* the earnings report at prices that prevailed *before* the report.

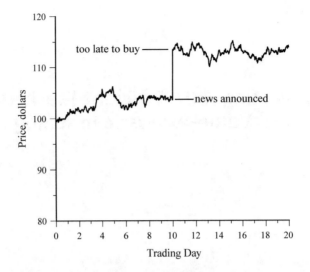

Fig. 4.1 An immediate reaction in an efficient market

On the other hand, we also noted in our Chapter 2 discussion of these Oracle and Apple examples that the market evidently overreacted in both cases in that *buying* after the price collapse turned out to be very profitable. These are not unique examples. The stock market often overreacts.

Gary looked at the daily returns on the stocks in the Dow Jones Industrial Average back to October 1, 1928, when the Dow was expanded from 20 to 30 stocks. He defined a "big day" for a Dow stock as a day when the stock's return was 5 percentage points higher or lower than the average return on the other 29 Dow stocks that day. (For a robustness check, Gary also looked at big-day cut-offs of 6, 7, 8, 9, or 10 percentage points and obtained similar results.)

Figure 4.2 shows the average cumulative returns for the big-day stocks compared to the other 29 stocks over the ten days after the big day. Large positive and (especially) negative returns tended to be followed by persistent, substantial, and statistically persuasive reversals over the next ten days. Overreaction tends to be more pronounced for bad news than for good news because investors are more susceptible to panic than lust.

When you are thinking about buying or selling a stock, it is good to remember the saying

What everybody knows isn't worth knowing.

The benchmark for gauging your investment ideas is not

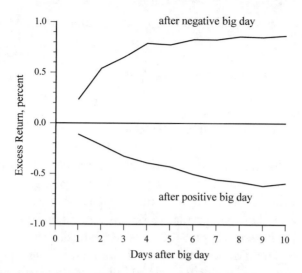

Fig. 4.2 Average cumulative excess returns after a big day

How is today different from yesterday?

or

How will tomorrow be different from today?

but

How will tomorrow be different from what others expect?

When you think you have a good reason for buying or selling a stock, ask yourself if you know something that other investors don't know. If you do, it may be inside information that is illegal to use. If you don't, your information may already be reflected in market prices.

Random Walks and $100 Bills on the Sidewalk

If stock prices take into account all available information, then they are only affected by new information—and new information is, by definition, unpredictable. If it was predictable, it wouldn't be news!

This argument implies stock prices follow a *random walk* much like a very drunk person whose next step cannot be predicted from previous steps. If stock prices wander randomly, then trying to beat the market by predicting which way stock prices will go next is a waste of time. As the Danish proverb reminds us:

It is difficult to make predictions, especially about the future.

There is a famous parable about two finance professors who see a $100 bill on the sidewalk. As one professor reaches for it, the other says, "Don't bother; if it was real, someone would have picked it up by now." Finance professors are fond of saying that the stock market doesn't leave $100 bills on the sidewalk, meaning that there are never obvious profits for the taking.

There is truth in that, but it is not completely true. Stock prices are sometimes wacky. During speculative booms and financial crises, the stock market leaves suitcases full of $100 bills on the sidewalk. Still, when you think you have found an easy way to make money, you should ask yourself if other investors have overlooked a $100 bill on the sidewalk or if you have overlooked a logical explanation.

Thinking Clearly

There is an important distinction between *possessing* information and *processing* information. Possessing information is knowing something others do not know. Processing information is thinking clearly about things we all know.

Stock prices depend not only on known facts, but also human emotions—like greed and overconfidence—that lead some investors astray. Warren Buffett did not beat the market for decades by having access to information that was not available to others, but by thinking more clearly about information available to everyone.

In the 1980s Gary debated the efficient market hypothesis with a prominent Stanford professor. Gary said that Buffett's success was evidence that the market could be beaten by processing information better than other investors. The Stanford professor's response was immediate and dismissive, "Enough monkeys hitting enough keys...." He was referring to the classic infinite monkey theorem, one version of which states that if a very large number of monkeys pound away at typewriters, one will eventually write every book that humans have ever written. The Stanford professor's argument was that so many people have been buying and selling stocks over so many decades, that someone is bound to have been so much luckier than the rest as to appear to be a genius—when they are really just a lucky monkey.

In a 1984 speech at Columbia University celebrating the 50th anniversary of Benjamin Graham and David Dodd's value-investing treatise, *Security Analysis*, Buffett rebutted the lucky-monkey argument by noting that he personally knows eight other portfolio managers who, like Buffett, adhere to the value-investing principles taught by Graham and Dodd. All nine have outperformed the market dramatically for many years. How many monkeys would it take to generate that performance?

Yet, many academics are skeptical (or perhaps jealous?). In 2006, Austan Goolsbee, a Chicago Business School professor who served as Chair of the Council of Economic Advisers for President Obama, was interviewed on American Public Media and said,

> I'd tell [Berkshire Hathaway] shareholders to watch their wallets. See, I'm an economist, and it always sticks in my craw when people say Warren has the Midas Touch. That's because the one thing that professors pound into young economists is that the only investors who beat the market are ones who get lucky or else take risk.

We are unpersuaded. We have a personal interest in believing that some investors process information better than others, just as do some doctors and lawyers. Our belief in Buffett is fortified by the fact that, unlike monkeys, Buffett makes sense. His annual letters to Berkshire shareholders are exceptionally wise and well-written. We highly recommend reading them.

Buffett generally ignores the crowd and makes up his own mind. Other investors have prospered by watching the crowd and doing the opposite—by taking advantage of the tendency of stock prices to overreact. Bargains are not going to be found when investors are optimistic, but when they are pessimistic. In Buffett's memorable words, "Be fearful when others are greedy and greedy when others are fearful."

The Delusion of Crowds

A Harvard Business School professor wrote, "The vast scientific evidence on the theory of efficient markets indicates that, in the absence of inside information, a security's market price represents the best available estimate of its true value." The idea is that while some investors may substantially overestimate the value of a stock, other investors will err in the opposite direction and these errors will balance out so that the collective judgment of the crowd is close to the correct value.

The wisdom of crowds has a lot of appeal. The classic example is a jelly bean experiment conducted by finance professor Jack Treynor. He showed

56 students a jar containing 850 jelly beans and asked them to write down how many beans they thought were in the jar. The average guess was 871, an error of only 2%. Only one student did better. This experiment has been cited over and over as evidence that the average opinion of the value of a stock is likely to be close to the "true" value.

The analogy is not apt. As Treynor noted, the student guesses were evidently made independently and had no systematic bias. When these assumptions are true, the average guess will, on average, be closer to the true value than the majority of the individual guesses. That is a mathematical fact. But it is not a fact if the assumptions are wrong—if the guesses are biased and not independent.

After the initial student guesses were recorded, Treynor advised the class that they should allow for air space at the top of the bean jar and that the plastic jar's exterior was thinner than a normal glass jar. The average estimate increased to 979.2, an error of 15%. The many were no longer smarter than the few. Treynor wrote, "Although the cautions weren't intended to be misleading, they seem to have caused some shared error to creep into the estimates."

There is a lot of shared error in the stock market. Stock prices are buffeted by fads, fancies, greed, and gloom—what Keynes called "animal spirits." Contagious mass psychology causes not only pricing errors, but speculative bubbles and unwarranted panics.

Nobel Laureate Eugene Fama is one of the most prominent and influential proponents of the efficient market hypothesis. He described

> an 'efficient' market for securities, that is, a market where, given the available information, actual prices at every point in time represent very good estimates of intrinsic values.

Fama earned his Ph.D. and spent virtually his entire career teaching at the University of Chicago, a school known for its embrace of the power of markets. (Goolsbee is at Chicago, too.) Fama's argument is that if stock prices take into account all available information and are the best assessment of the true value of stocks, then changes in stock prices will be unpredictable. The extensive evidence on how difficult it is to predict stock prices therefore demonstrates that stock prices take into account all available information and are the best assessment of the true value of stocks.

That argument is superficially appealing but nonetheless a logical fallacy. A implies B does not mean that B implies A. It is like saying: all players in the English Premier League played soccer as youngsters; therefore, everyone who plays youth soccer will play in the Premier League.

Changes in stock prices may be hard to predict because of unpredictable, sometimes irrational, changes in investor moods and expectations. If so, short-term changes in market prices may be impossible to predict but market prices are not good estimates of intrinsic value. There is plenty of evidence that stock prices do sometimes depart from intrinsic values—most obviously during bubbles, some of which were recounted in Chapter 1. The dot-com and cryptocurrency bubbles are additional examples.

The Dot-Com Bubble

Back in the 1990s, when computers and cell phones were just starting to take over our lives, the spread of the Internet sparked the creation of hundreds of Internet-based companies, popularly known as dot-coms. Some dot-coms had good ideas and matured into strong, successful companies but many did not. In too many cases, the idea was simply to start a company with a dot-com in its name, sell it to someone else, and walk away with pockets full of cash. The dot-com fever was so hot that scoundrels were able to execute *rug pulls* by raising money with a promise to start a company and then disappearing, leaving investors flat on their backs and wondering where the heck their money went.

One study found that existing companies that simply added *.com*, *.net*, or *Internet* to their names more than doubled the price of their stock. That wouldn't have happened if market prices had been the best estimates of these companies' intrinsic values.

If investors had thought about stocks the way John Burr William, Ben Graham, and other value investors did, they would have noticed how little income was being generated by dot-com companies and they might have been skeptical rather than delirious. Instead, wishful investors closed their eyes to the absence of profits and thought up new metrics for the so-called New Economy. They argued that, instead of being obsessed with something as old fashioned as profits, we should look at the number of people who visited a website, the number who stayed for at least three minutes, or the number of files that websites downloaded from servers. Some said we should look at a company's burn rate, how fast it spent the money it had raised. The faster, the better!

Stock prices tripled between 1995 and 2000, an annual rate of increase of 25%. Dot-com stocks rose even more. The tech-heavy NASDAQ index more than quintupled during this five-year period, an annual rate of increase of 40%. Someone who bought $10,000 of AOL stock in January 1995 or Yahoo when it went public in April 1996 would have had nearly $1 million in January 2000.

Dot-com entrepreneurs and stock market investors were getting rich and they thought it would never end. But, of course, it did.

In an investor survey near the peak of the dot-com bubble in 2000, the median prediction of the annual return on stocks over the next ten years was 15%. It wasn't just naive amateurs. Supposedly sophisticated hedge funds were buying dot-com stocks just as feverishly as retail investors. This was not collective wisdom; this was collective delusion. They didn't see the bubble because they did not want to see it. The actual annual return over the next ten years turned out to be *negative* 0.5%.

The Cryptocurrency Bubble(s)

Cryptocurrencies are digital transaction records archived in decentralized blockchains which, in theory, preserve the anonymity of users. We will focus our attention on bitcoin, the original and most well-known cryptocurrency.

Bitcoin transactions are slow and expensive. The only reason to buy something with bitcoin instead of a credit card or checking account is to try to hide the transaction—perhaps because it is illegal or to avoid taxes. We now know that bitcoin creates an electronic trail that can help law enforcement officials follow the money and document criminal transactions.

Another problem with bitcoin transactions is that bitcoin prices are very volatile and may change substantially between when a transaction is started and when it is executed.

On the other hand, one person's problem is sometimes another person's opportunity. The wild gyrations in bitcoin prices have lured many into thinking that they can get rich speculating in bitcoin. Starting from a price of about a tenth of a penny in October 2009, bitcoin's price hit $1.00 in February 2011 and fluctuated wildly before hitting $100 in April 2013. The price topped $1,000 in January 2014 and then bottomed at $111.60 in February. Figure 4.3 shows the wild ups and downs in bitcoin prices since 2014.

Bitcoin is pure speculation. Bitcoin generates no income whatsoever, so its intrinsic value is a big fat zero. Tulip bulbs can at least be planted and multiply. Dot-com companies might actually generate profits. The only way to get anything out of a bitcoin "investment" is to sell it to a bigger fool.

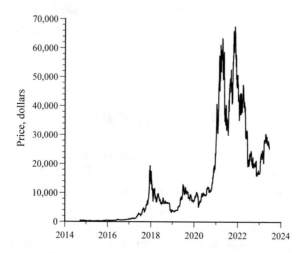

Fig. 4.3 The bitcoin roller coaster

The true nature of cryptocurrencies is well demonstrated by the fact that, as of March 2023, there were more than 23,000 cryptocurrencies. We certainly don't need tens of thousands of cryptocurrencies for buying and selling things and these tens of thousands of cryptocurrencies are not intended to buy or sell anything. A few, like Dogecoin, started as a prank. Almost all are essentially Ponzi schemes, intended to enrich the originators at the expense of fools hoping to find greater fools.

Unlike a classic bubble, the prices of bitcoin and other cryptocurrencies have soared and crashed several times. Just when the bubble seems to have popped, it inflates again. One explanation is that cryptocurrency exchanges are largely unregulated and there is considerable market manipulation, including repeated pump-and-dump schemes. Economics Nobel laureate Paul Krugman wrote, "Back in 2013 fraudulent activities by a single trader appear to have caused a sevenfold increase in Bitcoin's price." A study published in the *Journal of Finance* concluded that nearly all of the sharp run-up in bitcoin prices in 2017 was due to one large, unidentified trader using another digital currency, called Tether, to buy bitcoin. In 2019 the *Wall Street Journal* reported that nearly 95% of reported bitcoin transactions are sham trades used to manipulate prices. In a 2021 report, Research Affiliates, a widely respected investment management company, concluded,

> *perhaps [bitcoin] is just a bubble driven by a frenzy of retail, and some institutional, money eager to get a piece of the action. Alternatively, and far likelier in my opinion, is that this "bubble" is more fraud than frenzy.*

The SEC has said that cryptocurrency markets are "rife with fraud, scams and abuse" and, together with the U.S. Justice Department, has begun charging people and companies with a variety of civil and criminal charges.

Cryptocurrencies are a perfect example of a market in which prices are not the best estimate of intrinsic value.

The Performance of Professionals

One test of the efficient market hypothesis is whether professional money managers consistently outperform amateurs. If they do, then it evidently is possible to bet the market. We need to take risk into account in order to implement such tests and mean–variance analysis gave researchers a way to measure risk-adjusted performance.

Consider two professionally managed mutual funds, Fund 1 and Fund 2. Fund 1's annual return has averaged 10% with a standard deviation of

4 Investing 4.0—Efficient Markets and Value-Agnostic ...

10%, while Fund 2's annual return has averaged 20% with a standard deviation of 20%. Which performance is more impressive? We can use the fact, shown in Fig. 3.4 in Chapter 3, that when a safe asset (like Treasury bills) is combined with a risky asset (like a mutual fund), the mean/standard deviation possibilities are given by a straight line between the two investments.

Figure 4.4 shows these straight lines for our two hypothetical mutual funds, using a 5% annual return on safe 1-year Treasury bills. The lower line shows the possible combinations of Treasury bills and Fund 1. The upper line shows the possible combinations of Treasury bills and Fund 2. Fund 2 outperformed Fund 1 in that for any specified level of risk (as measured by the standard deviation), the average return from combining Fund 2 with Treasury bills exceeded that from combining Fund 1 with Treasury bills.

The dotted line in Fig. 4.4 illustrates this argument for a standard deviation of 6%. A 60/40 investment in Fund 1 and Treasury bills would have had a standard deviation of 6% and an average return of 8%. However, a 30/70 investment in Fund 2 and Treasury bills would have had a standard deviation of 6% and an average return of 9.5%. Similar logic applies for any specified standard deviation. Therefore, by this criterion, Fund 2 did better than Fund 1, even after taking risk into account.

Instead of having to draw a mean–variance diagram to see which fund did better, we can calculate the slopes of lines drawn from the Treasury-bill rate to the fund. The fund with the higher slope wins. In Fig. 4.4, Fund 2 wins

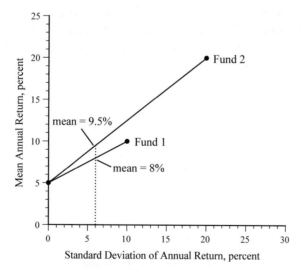

Fig. 4.4 Comparing two hypothetical mutual funds

because it has a higher slope. The slope, called the Sharpe Ratio, is

$$\text{Sharpe Ratio} = \frac{\text{average portfolio return} - \text{risk-free return}}{\text{portfolio standard deviation}}$$

The Sharpe ratio got its name from William F. Sharpe's 1966 study of the performance of professionally managed mutual funds. He found 34 stock mutual funds that had annual return data for all of the years 1944 through 1963. If anything, these returns overstated mutual fund performance. Sharpe took into account management fees and other expenses, but he did not take into account the "load fees" of approximately 8.5% that most of these funds charged for the privilege of investing in the fund. These data were also tainted by survivor bias in that poorly performing mutual funds tend to close or to be absorbed into other funds with their prior performance record expunged. The 34 funds that survived this 20-year period surely had better records than did the unknown number of funds that vanished without a trace.

Sharpe compared the annual returns of each of these 34 funds over the 10-year period 1954 through 1963 to the annual returns for the Dow Jones Industrial Average. To compare performances on a risk-adjusted basis, we can plot the Dow and the 34 funds just like we did for the two hypothetical funds in Fig. 4.4.

Figure 4.5 does this with a line drawn from an assumed 3% safe return to the Dow's performance. The slope of this line is the Dow's Sharpe ratio. The Sharpe ratios for the 34 mutual funds are the slopes of lines down from the safe asset to each fund's point in the graph. The Sharpe ratios of the 23 funds that are below the Dow line in Fig. 4.5 are lower than the Dow's Sharpe ratio. Thus, Sharpe concluded that the risk-adjusted performance of 23 of these 34 mutual funds was inferior to the Dow.

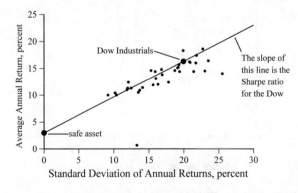

Fig. 4.5 Risk-adjusted performance of 34 mutual funds

4 Investing 4.0—Efficient Markets and Value-Agnostic ...

The returns in Fig. 4.5 take management fees and other expenses into account because it is the net returns that matter to investors. Sharpe also looked at fund performance before management fees and other expenses were deducted, and found that 19 funds did better and 15 funds did worse than the Dow. His conclusion was that professionally managed mutual funds, on average, do about as well as (or maybe somewhat better than) the market before management fees, but worse afterward. Therefore, professionally managed funds do not perform well enough to justify the fees they charge.

The Sharpe ratio is popular but it has all the problems of mean–variance analysis that we discussed in Chapter 3. We will reiterate two of these problems here. The first is that the Sharpe ratio gauges risk by the short-term volatility of prices rather than by long-run uncertainty about the income being generated by investments. Look again at Fig. 4.5 and imagine that there is an investment with a 4% average return and 1% standard deviation. It is well above the Dow line and its Sharpe ratio

$$\text{Sharpe Ratio} = \frac{\text{average portfolio return} - \text{risk-free return}}{\text{portfolio standard deviation}}$$
$$= \frac{4\% - 3\%}{1\%}$$
$$= 1.00$$

is far above the Dow's Sharpe ratio (0.67) and also higher than the highest Sharpe ratio of any of these 34 mutual funds (0.76). Yet, it would have been a truly awful investment over this 10-year period, giving a total return far below the Dow and also far below the worst of these 34 mutual funds.

A second problem is the reliance on historical data to gauge risk and return. In Chapter 3 we saw that past means and standard deviations are unreliable estimates of future means and standard deviations for individual stocks. Are historical estimates of mutual fund performance also unreliable? To investigate this question, Sharpe compared the Sharpe ratios for these 34 funds in the 10-year period 1944 through 1953 with their Sharpe ratios in the 10-year period 1954 through 1963. The correlation between the Sharpe ratios was 0.32, which is neither substantial or statistically persuasive. Even if the Sharpe ratio were a compelling measure of past performance, it is not a trustworthy barometer for evaluating future investment decisions.

Although the Sharpe ratio is deeply flawed, Sharpe's study of mutual fund performance is consistent with other studies that have concluded that the record of professional investors as a group has been mediocre, at best.

In his persuasive book, *The New Contrarian Investment Strategy*, David Dreman looked at 52 surveys of stocks or stock portfolios recommended by professional investors. Forty underperformed the market. Perhaps some professionals are pros and the rest are amateurs pretending to be pros. Nope. There is no consistency in which professional investors do well and which do poorly. A study of 200 institutional stock portfolios found that of those who ranked in the top 25% in one five-year period, 26% ranked in the top 25% during the next five years, 48% ranked in the middle 50%, and 26% were in the bottom 25%.

Indexing

As the evidence accumulated that professional money managers are not worth what they are being paid, index funds were created. If actively managed mutual funds do worse than the market, just buy the market.

John Bogle had written his senior thesis at Princeton on the failure of mutual funds to beat the S&P 500 and he drew the natural conclusion that the way to beat most mutual funds was to buy the stocks in the S&P 500. He wrote that mutual funds "may make no claim to superiority over the market averages" and that investor performance "can be maximized by reducing sales charges and management fees"—fire the highly paid fund managers and simply buy and hold the stocks in the market averages.

Bogle founded Vanguard in 1975 and, a year later, introduced the first index fund open to small investors. It did not go well. The fund's IPO had hoped to raise $250 million; it raised $11 million. Bogle's strategy became known as "Bogle's Folly." The head of Fidelity, the largest mutual fund group at the time, sniffed, "I can't believe that the great mass of investors are going to be satisfied with just receiving average returns."

Well, an average return is better than the below-average returns generated by most high-cost, actively managed funds. Vanguard has soared past Fidelity and become the world's largest mutual fund group as investors have come to appreciate the advantages of low-cost indexing. Nearly half of all mutual fund money is now invested in index funds.

The low-cost advantage is squandered when people pay financial advisors to put them in index funds. For instance, we have a relative ("Larry") who started a company several years ago that he sold for around $10 million. After interviewing several money managers, he chose one who charges 1% of assets under management and who invested Larry's entire $10 million in index funds. Even if the assets don't grow over time, Larry will pay this money manager $100,000 a year—$1 million over the next 10 years—to do what Larry can do on his own.

When we pointed this out to Larry, he shrugged his shoulders and said that it was a CYA strategy. If he invested the money himself and the stock market went down, his wife would give him two earsful. Now, he can just point to his money manager and say, "Honey, this is what the pros are doing."

Index funds are not a bad investment strategy but paying someone to invest your money in index funds is seldom a good idea.

Value-Agnostic Investing

Mean–variance analysis and indexing have, in many ways, undermined the value-investing insights of Investing 2.0. Mean–variance investors generally use historical stock return data to choose portfolios. There is no consideration whatsoever of dividends, earnings, and intrinsic values. Indexing dispenses with value investing entirely. In contrast to Benjamin Graham's depiction of Mr. Market as a fool, efficient market aficionados view Mr. Market as omniscient. Mean–variance analysis and indexing are both *value-agnostic* in that investors do not consider whether stock prices might be too high or too low relative to intrinsic values.

We acknowledge that many actively managed funds charge too much for too little. Overpromising and underdelivering is endemic. We respect and recommend Vanguard and other low-cost index funds. However, we are convinced that stock prices are sometimes driven far from intrinsic values by human emotions. Stocks are sometimes cheap. Stocks are sometimes expensive.

We also recognize the efficient market paradox. If nobody believed that markets are efficient, then investors would have an incentive to do careful research and stock prices might reflect this careful analysis—in which case, the argument would be strongest for investors *not* to do research. On the other hand, if everyone believed that the stock market is efficient, then no one would bother doing research—in which case, the argument would be strongest for investors to do careful research.

For many, indexing is a low-cost way to invest in stocks. To the extent that indexing encourages people to buy stocks instead of keeping cash in safes and checking accounts or speculating on precious metals and cryptocurrencies, index funds are a low-cost blessing. In addition, value-agnostic investing loosens the ties between market prices and intrinsic value, which is also a blessing—for value investors.

The next innovation in investment strategies—what we call Investing 5.0—is far nuttier than indexing. It is a completely fantastical theory that measures risk poorly and creates additional lucrative opportunities for value investors.

References

Basu, S. 1977. Investment performance of common stocks in relation to their price-earnings ratios: A test of the efficient market hypothesis, *Journal of Finance*, 32, 663–682.

Bogle, John C. 1995. *Bogle on Mutual Funds*, Burr Ridge, IL: Irwin.

Buffett, Warren. 1984. The Superinvestors of Graham-and-Doddsville, *Hermes, The Columbia Business School Magazine*, Fall, 4–15.

Cooper, Michael J., Dimitrov, Orlin, and Rau, P. Raghavendra. 2001, A rose.com by any other name, *Journal of Finance*, 56, 2371–2388.

DeBondt, W. F. M., and Thaler, R. 1985. Does the stock market overreact?, *Journal of Finance*, 40, 793–805.

DeBondt, W. F. M., and Thaler, R. 1987. Further evidence on investor overreaction and stock market seasonality, *Journal of Finance*, 42, 557–580.

Dreman, David. 1982. *The New Contrarian Investment Strategy*, New York: Random House.

Dreman, David, and Berry, M. A. 1995. Analysts forecasting errors and their implications for security analysis, *Financial Analysts Journal*, 51, 30–40.

Dunn, Patricia C., and Theisen, Rolf D. 1983. How consistently do active managers win?, *Journal of Portfolio Management*, Summer, 47–50.

Fama, Eugene F. 1965. The behavior of stock market prices, *Journal of Business*, 38(1), 34–105.

Fama, Eugene F. 1991. Efficient capital markets: II, *Journal of Finance*, 46, 1575–1617.

Fama, Eugene F., and French, Kenneth R. 1988. Permanent and temporary components of stock prices, *Journal of Political Economy*, 96(2), 246–273.

Garrett, Thomas A., and Sobel, Russell S. 1999. Gamblers favor skewness, not risk: Further evidence from United States lottery games, *Economics Letters*, 63(1), 85–90.

Golec, Josept, and Tamarkin, Maurry. 1998. Bettors love skewness, not risk, at the horse track, *Journal of Political Economy*, 106(1), 205–225.

Goolsbee, Austin. 2006. Interviewed by Kai Ryssdal, *American Public Media*, May 5.

Griffin, John M., and Shams, Amin. 2020. Is Bitcoin really un-tethered?, *The Journal of Finance*, 75(4), 1913–1964.

Keynes, John Maynard. 1936. *The General Theory of Employment, Interest, and Money*, New York: Macmillan, Chapter 12.

Krugman, Paul. 2018. Bubble, Bubble, Fraud and Trouble, *The New York Times*, January 29.
Kumar, A., 2009. Who gambles in the stock market?, *The Journal of Finance*, 64(4), 1889–1933.
Mitton, Todd, and Vorkink, Keith. 2007. Equilibrium underdiversification and the preference for skewness. *Review of Financial Studies*, 20(4), 1255–1288.
Pickard, Alex. 2012. Bitcoin: Magic Internet Money, Research Affiliates.
Rosenberg, B., Reid, K., and Lanstein, R. 1985. Persuasive evidence of market inefficiency, *Journal of Portfolio Management*, 11, 9–17.
Sharpe, W. F. 1966. Mutual Fund Performance, *Journal of Business*, 39, 119–138.
Smith, Gary. 2016. Overreaction of Dow Stocks, *Cogent Economics & Finance*, 4(1), 1251831.
Treynor, Jack. 1987. Market Efficiency and the Bean Jar Experiment, *Financial Analysts Journal*, 43, 50–53.
Vigna, Paul. 2019. Most Bitcoin Trading Faked by Unregulated Exchanges, Study Finds, *Wall Street Journal*, March 22.

5

Investing 5.0—Factor Models, Algorithms, and Chasing Alpha

The development of mean–variance analysis in the 1950s was followed in the 1960s by the Capital Asset Pricing Model (CAPM), which gives a more sophisticated measure of risk but is an unfortunate detour away from value investing because it focuses on short-term price fluctuations.

Portfolio theory advises that risk can be reduced by selecting a diversified portfolio of stocks. What if all investors follow this advice? Which stocks are genuinely risky if all stocks are held in diversified portfolios? A stock's portfolio riskiness depends on how its return is correlated with the returns on other stocks. A stock that does poorly when other stocks do poorly is risky because it offers very little diversification benefits. A stock that does well when other stocks do poorly reduces portfolio risk. Therefore, a valid measure of a stock's portfolio risk should take into account the correlation of its return with the returns on other stocks.

The Capital Asset Pricing Model (CAPM)

CAPM does this. This is another of those finance models that makes wildly unrealistic assumptions, uses impressive math, yields remarkable insights, and should be applied with caution. The CAPM logic applies to all investments, but it is most commonly applied to stocks and, for simplicity, we will do that, too.

CAPM assumes that all investors: (1) can borrow and lend at an interest rate equal to the Treasury-bill rate; (2) choose their portfolios using mean–variance analysis; and (3) agree on the values of all of the means, variances, and correlations that determine the unique optimal stock portfolio given by Tobin's separation theorem. Therefore, every investor chooses this optimal stock portfolio, making it the market portfolio. If every investor has twice as much money invested in XXX than in YYY, then the total market value of XXX must be twice the market value of YYY.

Talk about wildly unrealistic assumptions! Investors cannot borrow and lend at the Treasury-bill rate. Not all investors use mean–variance analysis. Those investors who use mean–variance analysis do not agree on the means, variances, and correlations. Everyone does not hold the same stock portfolio. The huge volume of daily trading in stocks is ample evidence of investor disagreement—which is ruled out in CAPM.

Nonetheless, the CAPM conclusion that the market portfolio is the optimal portfolio fits well with the efficient market hypothesis. Indeed, it is this synchronization of mean–variance analysis, CAPM, and the efficient market hypothesis that led the field of finance into its current morass, neglecting the insights of value investing.

We will spare you the impressive math that leads to this remarkable CAPM equation which states that the excess return on any stock (relative to the risk-free rate) is proportional to the overall market's excess return,

$$E - R_0 = \beta(E_M - R_0) \tag{5.1}$$

where E is the expected return on an individual stock, E_M is the expected return on the market as a whole, and R_0 is the return on a risk-free asset like Treasury bills.

The coefficient β ("beta") in Eq. 5.1 is the slope of a line, as in Fig. 5.1, describing the relationship between a stock's return and the overall market return. The idea is that there are common macroeconomic factors like the strength of the economy and interest rates that affect all stocks, but some stocks are affected more than others. A stock with a slope of, say, $\beta = 0.8$, means that this stock is less sensitive to macroeconomic factors than are most stocks. If macroeconomic events cause the market return to increase by 10%, the return on this stock is predicted to increase by only 8%.

In practice, fluctuations in short-term stock returns are almost entirely due to fluctuations in stock prices. So, a 0.8 beta coefficient means that if the stock market goes up 10%, the price of this stock is expected to go up 8%.

Figure 5.2 shows a scatter diagram of the monthly returns for Apple and the S&P 500 during the five-year period 2005 through 2009. The slope of the best-fit line is 1.54. This 1.54 beta coefficient indicates that Apple stock tends to move with the overall market, but much more than the market. Specifically, if the market goes up 10% one month, Apple stock is predicted

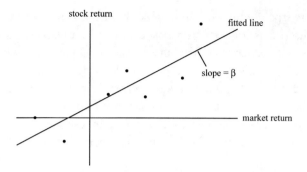

Fig. 5.1 The beta coefficient gauges how a stock return is related to the overall market

to go up 15.4% that month; if the market goes down 10% one month, Apple is predicted to go down 15.4%.

The average beta for all stocks is 1. Stocks with betas above one are riskier than average and, according to Eq. 5.1, have above-average expected returns. Stocks with betas below one have below-average risk and below-average expected returns. Here is a simple summary:

$$E - R_0 = \beta(E_M - R_0)$$
$$E > E_M \quad \text{if } \beta > 1$$
$$E = E_M \quad \text{if } \beta = 1$$
$$E = 0 \quad \text{if } \beta = 0$$

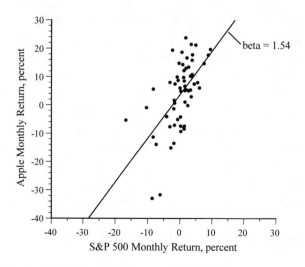

Fig. 5.2 Apple and S&P 500 monthly returns, 2005–2009

A zero-beta stock, which might be risky by itself, adds nothing to portfolio risk. All of its risk is idiosyncratic risk that can be diversified away. A zero-beta stock is not riskier than Treasury bills if it is part of a well-diversified portfolio—which it always is in the CAPM model—so people will hold a zero-beta stock even though its expected return is the same as Treasury bills. A negative-beta stock is even safer because it tends to do well when other investments do poorly. It will be held by risk-averse investors even if the expected return is less than Treasury bills. In practice, very few stocks have negative betas.

The empirical evidence strongly rejects the CAPM model (Eq. 5.1). High-beta stocks do not do as well, on average, as they should, and low-beta stocks do better than they should. Nonetheless, some investors find betas useful for assessing the riskiness of their portfolios and for wagering on the overall stock market.

Betting with Betas

Investors who believe that the stock market is about to go up can put their money where their mouths are by loading up on high-beta stocks. Investors who fear the market is about to go down can try to make their portfolio less vulnerable to a market crash by shifting to low-beta stocks.

Our issue with such strategies is that they are a misguided return to the Investing 1.0 foolishness of trying to predict short-term swings in stock prices. Consider an investor at the beginning of 2010 who is bullish on the stock market. Going through a list of betas estimated from monthly data for 2005 through 2009, this investor is attracted to Apple because it has a beta of 1.54. The investor then buys Apple and other high-beta stocks, not because the price of Apple is reasonable relative to its intrinsic value but because the investor has a hunch that the overall market is about to go up.

Apple's beta coefficient has nothing whatsoever to do with whether Apple stock is a bargain or a bubble. Those who bet with betas never consider the question of whether Apple's stock price is too high, too low, or about right. Using monthly betas, all they care about is monthly price fluctuations.

Even worse, for reasons we will discuss soon, beta coefficients are not set in stone. Apple's beta for the five years 2005 through 2009 was 1.54 but its beta coefficient for the next five years, 2010 through 2014, turned out to be 0.92—Apple tended to move *less* than the market. For the five years after that, 2015 through 2019, Apple's beta was back up to 1.25.

Chasing Alpha

The CAPM equation

$$E - R_0 = \beta(E_M - R_0)$$

applies not only to individual stocks but also to stock portfolios, including portfolios that might be chosen as part of a beat-the-market strategy. Such strategies can be tested by using performance data to estimate this equation

$$R - R_0 = \alpha + \beta(R_M - R_0) \qquad (5.2)$$

where R is the observed portfolio return and R_M is the observed market return.

According to the CAPM equation, α ("alpha") should be zero. If the performance data yield an estimated value of alpha that is positive, this is evidence that the strategy has beaten the market, taking risk into account. If alpha is negative, the strategy underperformed the market. If, for example, monthly data give an alpha estimate of 0.2%, that is a 0.2% monthly excess return (which is approximately a 2.4% annual excess return).

The sensible idea is that since high-beta stocks should have above-average returns, we don't want to credit a strategy with "beating the market" when all it did was load up on high-beta stocks. The interesting and relevant question is whether a strategy beats the market, taking into account the strategy's beta. Equation 5.2 (above) answers that question.

This idea is so sensible that it is now standard practice to test strategies by estimating Eq. 5.2 and seeing whether the alpha estimate is positive, substantial, and statistically significant. Indeed, alpha has become part of the language of Wall Street. Investors might ask a portfolio manager, "What's your alpha?" A money manager might say, "Our annual alpha is 3 percent." Investment advisors and funds that want to not-so-subtly suggest that they beat the market include "alpha" in their name; for example, Alpha Diversified Fund, Alpha Capital Management, and Alpha Investment Consulting Group.

We hope that you can anticipate some of our objections to using alpha as a measure of investment success. In Chapter 3, we discussed various weaknesses of the mean–variance model that underlies CAPM. Later in this chapter, we will discuss several additional problems that CAPM adds to the weaknesses of mean–variance analysis.

Our fundamental objection is very simple. A persuasive investment goal should be to pursue a strategy that generates a long-run stream of income that is worth the cost. The relevant risk is that the income stream will turn out to be far less than anticipated.

The CAPM model instead assumes that risk is best gauged by the short-run volatility of stock prices, specifically the extent to which a stock's price is predicted to fluctuate when the stock market rises and falls. If a stock's price is expected to go up or down by 1.54% when the stock market goes up or down 1%, this stock is considered to be very risky. CAPM, like mean–variance analysis, assumes that investors care more about short-run price volatility than about long-run disappointments in the income from their investments.

Multiple-Factor Models

The CAPM beta coefficients are intended to reflect the fact that all stocks are affected, to varying degrees, by macroeconomic events that affect the overall stock market and also by idiosyncratic events specific to each company. This distinction is important because idiosyncratic risk can be diversified away but macroeconomic risks cannot. The only way to reduce macro risk is to hold low-beta stocks, which is why high-beta stocks must have above-average expected returns in order to attract risk-averse investors.

CAPM is an elegant theory—rewarded with Nobel prizes—that makes the worthwhile distinction between macro and idiosyncratic risks but it is too simple, by far, in that it assumes that there is just one macro factor—the overall stock market. The reality is that the stock market is affected by at least two distinct macroeconomic factors: the economy and interest rates. Some stocks, such as amusement parks, are very sensitive to the economy, while other stocks, such as savings and loan associations (S&Ls), are more sensitive to interest rates. When the overall stock market rises, will amusement parks or S&Ls go up more? It depends on *why* the market is booming. Is it because of a strong economy or because of falling interest rates?

If the market is booming because of falling interest rates, S&Ls have large beta coefficients. If the market is being propelled by a strong economy with stable interest rates, S&Ls have low beta coefficients. Figure 5.3 shows rolling estimates of the beta coefficient for First Financial Fund, a mutual fund that invested in small banks, savings institutions, and other financial firms. Each month, its beta was estimated from monthly data for the previous five years. First Financial was founded in 1986, so its first five-year beta estimate is at the beginning of January 1991 using data that go back to the beginning of January 1986. The estimates ended in 2010 when First Financial was

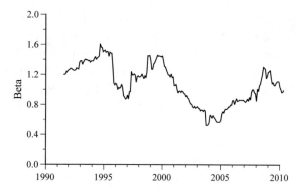

Fig. 5.3 First Financial Fund five-year betas, 1991–2010

delisted from the New York Stock Exchange after it was restructured to allow substantial investments in hedge funds.

If you bought First Financial in 1995, 2000, or 2010, thinking it was a high-beta stock, you would have been disappointed over the next several years. If you bought First Financial in 1996, 2003 or 2004, thinking it was a low-beta stock, you would have been disappointed, too.

This is a specific example of the more general point that a stock's beta coefficient depends on *why* the stock market goes up or down.

The problem—not just for S&Ls, but for all stocks—is that we have at least two macro factors and need at least two beta coefficients, one for the economy and one for interest rates. We can expand Eq. 5.2 to include several factors, thereby becoming a multiple-factor model. The first factor might be the unemployment rate or some other measure of the strength of the economy; its beta coefficient tells the effect of the unemployment rate on a particular stock's return. A second factor might be a long-term interest rate (such as the 10-year Treasury rate), with its beta coefficient gauging the effect of this interest rate on the stock's return.

Researchers can include as many factors as they think important—unemployment, interest rates, inflation, oil prices, tax rates, and so on. Unfortunately, this invitation to add factors has been grossly abused.

Anomalies

Shortly after the efficient market hypothesis became popular, researchers began accumulating evidence of so-called anomalies—investment strategies that beat the market even after taking risk into account (they had positive alphas).

For example, several studies found that companies with a small total market value ("small-cap stocks") have significantly outperformed other stocks. A plausible explanation is that it is not profitable for large financial institutions to do expensive research on small companies, because any attempt to buy a substantial number of shares will drive the price up and a later sale will force the price down. If small-cap stocks are neglected, they may also be cheap.

Several other studies found that out-of-favor stocks—as gauged by their low stock prices relative to their dividends, earnings, or book value have outperformed stocks with relatively high prices. If herd-like investors overreact to good or bad news, then it may pay to do the opposite of what the crowd is doing. This can be thought of as a contrarian strategy or a value-investing strategy using simple benchmarks.

The Fama–French Three-Factor Model

In 1992 Eugene Fama and Ken French reported that they had considered a variety of anomalies and concluded that differences among stock returns are related not only to the market factor used in CAPM, but also to a firm's size and the ratio of its book value to market value. This has become known as the Fama–French three-factor model:

$$R - R_0 = \alpha + \beta_1(R_M - R_0) + \beta_2 \text{SMB} + \beta_3 \text{HML} \qquad (5.3)$$

where
   $R - R_0$ = return on an individual stock minus return on Treasury bills
   $R_M - R_0$ = return on market portfolio minus return on Treasury bills
   SMB = size factor (small-cap stocks tend to do well)
   HML = value factor (stocks with high book values relative to market prices tend to do well)

The Fama–French three-factor model is the CAPM model with two additional factors. As with CAPM, it can be applied to investment strategies with the alpha coefficient assessing how well the strategy does, taking these three factors into account. Specifically, alpha is intended to gauge whether a strategy's observed performance is simply a reflection of a portfolio that overweighs high CAPM beta stocks, small-cap stocks, and value stocks. Whenever either of us writes a paper that discusses an investment strategy, the journal editors invariably expect to see alpha estimates using either CAPM, the Fama–French model, or both. We comply even though we think alpha estimates are a distraction.

You might think that Fama's confirmation of these small-cap and value anomalies would shake his faith in the efficient market hypothesis. If so, you would be wrong. Small-cap stocks and value stocks are not more volatile than the overall market yet Fama argues that, because markets are efficient (might as well assume what you are trying to prove), the above-average performance of small-cap stocks and value stocks shows that they must have risks that we may not understand but investors fear.

Dimensional Fund Advisors (DFA)

In 1981 three of Fama's former students (David Booth, Rex Sinquefield, and Larry Klotz) started an investment company named Dimensional Fund Advisors (DFA), which advertises itself as, "Applying rigorous academic research to practical investment solutions." DFA's core product is funds emphasizing the Fama–French factors, based on the presumption that small-cap stocks and value stocks will continue to deliver above-average returns.

DFA has maintained close links with the University of Chicago. Fama is a long-time DFA director and gives talks and writes articles for DFA though he continues to argue that the market portfolio is the most efficient portfolio and strategies that tilt away from the market portfolio are taking on additional risks. In 2008 Booth pledged $300 million to Chicago's business school, which is now named the University of Chicago Booth School of Business.

For many years, the only way that people could invest in a DFA fund was through a DFA-approved investment advisor. The lengthy advisor certification process included questionnaires, interviews, and attendance at a two-day conference where DFA representatives preached the DFA gospel. DFA-approved advisors must promise that they will never tell their clients to try to beat the market by buying individual stocks or by trying to time the market. In November 2020, DFA relaxed its grip a bit by introducing exchange-traded funds (ETFs) that allow people to invest in DFA funds directly without going through a DFA-authorized advisor.

Margaret attended a DFA advisor-screening conference and soon noticed the tension between DFA's ardent claim that the stock market is efficient and its simultaneous assertion that DFA funds beat the market by using factors that academics have identified as market beaters. This tension also shows up on its website. On the one hand, we have this efficient market perspective:

> At Dimensional, our investment approach is based on a belief in markets. Rather than attempting to predict the future or outguess others, we draw information about

expected returns from the market itself—leveraging the collective knowledge of its millions of buyers and sellers as they set security prices.

However, the website also proclaims that DFA has been, "Going beyond indexing since 1981" by using factors: "Research has shown that securities offering higher expected returns share certain characteristics, which we call dimensions."

DFA's first fund was the U.S. Micro Cap Portfolio, which was inspired by the small-cap factor. This fund currently invests at least 80% of its assets in small-cap stocks, while also taking into account the value factor and other factors that DFA has identified as market beaters. How has the fund done? Since its inception on December 23, 1981, through March 31, 2023, it has generated an annual return of 11.34%, which sounds great. However, over that same period, the annual return from the S&P 500 has been 11.60%. That 0.26% differential doesn't sound large but, compounded over 41-plus years, it is large. An initial $10,000 investment in DFA's US Micro Cap fund would have grown to $847,530 on March 31, 2023, while an investment in the S&P 500 would have grown to $934,272.

DFA launched the Japanese Small Company Portfolio in 1986, the United Kingdom Small Company Portfolio in 1986, and the Continental Small Company Portfolio (European companies) in 1988. If the argument is that small-cap companies are cheap because they are largely ignored, then that argument is even stronger for small-cap companies in Japan, the United Kingdom, and Switzerland. Alas, these international small-cap funds have done even worse than the U.S. Micro Cap Portfolio. The Japanese fund has underperformed the S&P 500 by an astonishing 5.83% a year, while the UK and Continental funds underperformed by 2.46 and 1.53%, respectively.

DFA now has nearly 150 funds—not only stock funds but also bonds, real estate, and commodities. It even has 13 target-date retirement funds which, as we will explain in Chapter 6, are generally bad ideas in and of themselves, with or without factors. Overall, of DFA's 89 pure stock funds, 18 of 34 US-based funds have underperformed the S&P 500, as have 48 of 55 international funds.

What happened? Maybe the academically endorsed factors were transitory correlations. Maybe the subsequent popularity of small-cap stocks made them no longer cheap. All we can say for certain is that factor investing does not guarantee profits. DFA's disappointing performance is, in fact, compelling evidence of the fragility and limited usefulness of CAPM and other factor models.

Notwithstanding its lackluster performance, DFA is now one of the world's largest fund families. Inspired by the success of DFA, factor (or "smart-beta") investing has become very popular and is now employed by many large money managers and embraced by individual investors who flock to factor funds.

Factors, Factors, Everywhere

In addition to the three Fama–French factors, other studies identified a momentum factor (stocks that have been doing well tend to keep doing well). In 2015, Fama and French added two more factors: a profitability factor (stocks of profitable companies tend to do well) and an investment factor (stocks of companies that invest conservatively tend to do well).

An interesting feature of these two additional factors is the utter implausibility of the idea that firms that are profitable and invest conservatively are somehow riskier than firms that are unprofitable and invest aggressively. Yet, Fama persists in arguing that, since markets are efficient, these factors must be proxies for risks that have not yet been identified.

Finding factors is not a difficult task. Hundreds of factors have been identified and more are reported all the time. The vast majority are rubbish, nothing more than coincidental correlations that are useless for predicting future returns. Resolute searches through historical data will inevitably turn up some variables that are correlated with stock prices. Even random numbers can be statistically significant factors.

Factors can even be found for bitcoin and other cryptocurrencies. A National Bureau of Economic Research (NBER) study published in a prestigious finance journal reported that past bitcoin returns could be "predicted" by several factors, including stock prices in these three industries:

> Paperboard Containers and Boxes
> Soaps, Cleaners, and Toilet Goods
> Cutlery, Hand Tools, and Hardware

These make no sense and the NBER authors didn't try to make sense of them: "We don't give explanations, we just document this behavior." They didn't really document behavior; they documented coincidences. They looked at literally hundreds of possible factors and some were bound to be coincidentally correlated with bitcoin returns.

For those who are tempted to think that there are logical explanations for the three factors listed above, Gary considered 100 clearly silly factors for predicting bitcoin prices: the daily high and low temperatures in fifty small cities with memorable names. He found a really good statistical fit with these 10 factors:

> Low temperature in Brunswick, Georgia
> Low temperature in Curtin Aero, Australia
> High temperature in Devils Lake, North Dakota
> Low temperature in Lincoln, Montana
> Low temperature in Moab Canyonland Airport, Utah
> Low temperature in Murphy, Idaho
> High temperature in Ohio Gulch, Idaho
> Low temperature in Quebec City Jean Lesange Airport
> Low temperature in Sanborn, Iowa
> Low temperature in Waterford City, North Dakota

Even though the daily temperatures in these ten cities have absolutely nothing to do with bitcoin prices, Fig. 5.4 shows the close fit between the actual daily bitcoin prices in 2015 and the prices predicted by the model. The correlation between actual and predicted bitcoin prices is a remarkable 0.82.

If an investment advisor showed you Fig. 5.4, would you be tempted to invest? We hope you recognize the peril of relying on past correlations and, at the very least, ask what these factors are. Unfortunately, many investment algorithms these days are black box, so no one, not even the programmers, knows which factors the algorithm has selected to make its predictions.

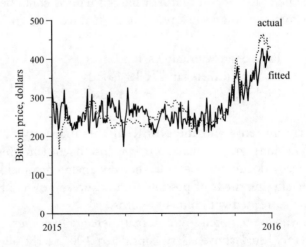

Fig. 5.4 Backtesting is spectacular

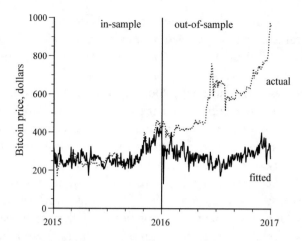

Fig. 5.5 Forecasting is awful

Of course, *prediction* is a misnomer. The model is "predicting" only in the sense of curve-fitting the past. The real test is how well the model predicts bitcoin prices for data that were not used to choose the factors. The answer, as with most factor models, is that factors chosen on the basis of past correlations are not reliable predictors of the future. Figure 5.5 shows the model's big whiff in 2016. The correlation is −0.002, negative but so close to zero as to be meaningless.

It is not surprising that factor investing has disappointed in recent years, even for the Fama–French factors. The overriding problem is that too many are too quick to assume that correlations that are found in historical data must be meaningful. No matter how often or how loudly statisticians shout that correlation is not causation, the deaf do not hear.

More Historical Data Will Not Help

Factor models ignore value-investing principles. They are similar to mean–variance models in that they focus on short-term changes in stock prices and neglect intrinsic values. When the models flop, they blame the data instead of the model.

Fama—the efficient market enthusiast and factor model proponent—has lamented that it is difficult to estimate probability distributions for stock prices because we only have reliable data on individual stock returns going back to 1926, which is less than 100 years of annual data and fewer than 25,000 daily observations. Few companies have been around that entire time, so the data set is even smaller than that.

What Fama revealed with his lament is the ill-founded presumption that future stock returns can be modeled reliably from historical data—if only we had more historical data. Really? Would stock returns from the nineteenth century be of any real relevance for valuing stocks in the twenty-first century? We can seldom see the future by looking in a rear-view mirror, let alone squinting through a telescope aimed at the wrong targets in the distant past.

Even if we had ten times as much data, we saw in Chapter 3 that it is very misleading to assume that stock returns can be modeled as random draws from a probability distribution or from slips of paper in a hat.

In a 2022 interview, Fama explicitly said, "I don't know what to use except for the historical average return." How about intrinsic value analysis? Instead of making investment decisions based on the use of past short-run price changes to predict future short-run price changes, how about estimating intrinsic values based on projected corporate profits and dividends?

Plundering Data

Factor models have become in many ways a subset of technical analysis—the ransacking of historical data for buy/sell signals based on statistical patterns. Millions of investors have spent billions of hours trying to discover formulas for beating the stock market. It is not surprising that some have stumbled on rules that explain the past remarkably well but fail to predict the future. Many such systems would be laughable, except for the fact that people believe in them.

Analysts have monitored sunspots, the water level of the Great Lakes, and sales of aspirin and yellow paint. Some believe that the market does especially well in years ending in *5* (1975, 1985, and so on) while others argue that years ending in *8* are best. Burton Crane, a long-time *New York Times* financial columnist, reported that a man, "ran a fairly successful investment advisory service based on his 'readings' of the comic strips in *The New York Sun*." *Money* magazine once reported that a Minneapolis stock broker selected stocks by spreading the *Wall Street Journal* on the floor and buying the stock touched by the first nail on the right paw of his golden retriever. The fact that he thought this would attract investors says something about him—and his customers.

The data deluge and powerful computers have made it incredibly easy to find patterns that are seductive but useless. Nearly a third of all U.S. stock trades are now made by black-box algorithms ("algos") that rummage through economic and noneconomic data, social media communications, and the price of tea in China, looking for correlations with stock prices. Algorithmic trading is technical analysis on steroids and has the same basic flaws, even though they might be hidden inside a mysterious black box.

There is no way to tell whether concealed black-box patterns make any sense. What we do know is that there are an essentially unlimited number of useless patterns waiting to be discovered—so, the chances that a randomly chosen pattern will be useful is very close to zero.

Mindless Algorithms

In 2017 a mutual fund group named Horizons launched the Active AI Global Equity Fund with the alluring ticker symbol MIND:

> *an investment strategy entirely run by a proprietary and adaptive artificial intelligence system that analyzes data and extracts patterns....The machine learning process underpinning MIND's investment strategy is known as* Deep Neural Network Learning—*which is a construct of artificial neural networks that enable the A.I. system to recognize patterns and make its own decisions, much like how the human brain works, but at hyper-fast speeds.*

Steve Hawkins, President and CEO, added that "Unlike today's portfolio managers who may be susceptible to investor biases such as overconfidence or cognitive dissonance, MIND is devoid of all emotion."

Not only is the fund devoid of all emotion, but it is also devoid of all intelligence. Despite the AI jargon, MIND is no more than a black-box algorithm searching for statistical patterns. The early returns were disappointing, but Hawkins suggested that these below-market returns increased the chances of above-market returns in the future:

> *To the extent that they may have underperformed today, there is a strong possibility that they can outperform in the future.*

This is the fallacious law of averages—the erroneous belief that every coin flip that lands heads makes tails more likely on the next flip—when, in reality, each coin flip is doggedly independent of previous flips.

When we are talking about human performance, past failures may be meaningful, but they do not, by themselves, make future successes more likely. We are reminded of a letter to columnist Marilyn vos Savant:

During the last year, I've gone on a lot of job interviews but I haven't been able to get a decent job....Doesn't the low of averages work here?

When we experience a series of disappointments, we may well hope that we are due for a change in fortune. It is unlikely that our disappointments will continue forever, but every failure does not make success more probable. Job applicants who are repeatedly rejected may need to apply for different jobs or improve their interview techniques.

In the same way, a mutual fund's below-market returns do not make above-market returns more likely. It may need new managers or a new strategy.

Figure 5.6 shows that MIND's initial underperformance was not a reason for optimism but a preview of what was to come. From its 2017 launch until the spring of 2022, MIND investors had a −10% return while those who invested in an S&P 500 index fund had a + 63% return. With MIND on life support, Horizons pulled the plug and terminated the fund on May 20, 2022.

Our intention is not to pick on this particular fund but to use its disappointing history to illustrate how the search for patterns in historical data—either by hand or by algorithm—is seductive but often disappointing.

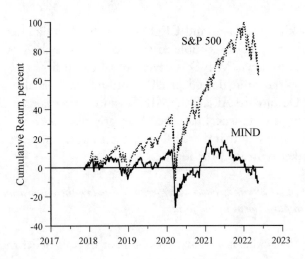

Fig. 5.6 Artificial unintelligence

Once Again, Mismeasuring Risk and Creating Opportunities

Mean–variance analysis, CAPM, factor models, and black-box algorithms all lure investors away from value investing because they focus on short-term price movements. Value investors don't try to predict short-term changes in stock prices. Nor do they look for factors that might cause short-term wiggles and jiggles in stock prices. Nor do they unleash black-box algorithms to search for statistical patterns that might be used to forecast zigs and zags in stock prices. They look forward, not backward, and they look at a company's cash flow, not its dancing stock price. Value investors know that the real risk is that their cash-flow projections may turn out to be overly optimistic.

Too many investors worry that a stock's price might dip right after they buy it. Don't be paralyzed by such fears. Price dips are not that important in the long run and it is nearly impossible to make reliable predictions of short-run price movements.

More important is a consideration of whether a stock's price is high or low relative to its intrinsic value. In theory, *any* decision to buy or sell *anything* should depend on its price. At some prices, apples are too expensive; at other prices, apples are a bargain. The same is true of stocks, at some prices, any stock—no matter how terrific or terrible—is too expensive; at other prices, it is a bargain. Yet, the practical effect of modern portfolio theory, indexing, CAPM, factor models, and algorithmic investing is that they never consider whether a stock's price might be too high, too low, or just about right in relation to the stock's intrinsic value. They focus on possible future price changes rather than actual current price levels.

Mean–variance models look at the means, variances, and correlations of historical *changes* in stock prices without any consideration whatsoever of the current *level* of stock prices. Index funds mechanically buy whichever stocks are in the index they are tracking, again with no attempt to assess whether stocks—in general or individually—are cheap or expensive. CAPM, factor-investing funds, and algorithmic investing models make no attempt to compare market prices with intrinsic values. They are all *value-agnostic*. The fortuitous consequence of these value-agnostic investment strategies is that they can create opportunities for value investors.

In addition, none of these models measure risk appropriately. Value investors assess investments by the income they generate. The most important risk is that the income will turn out to be disappointing. Instead of fretting about short-term price uncertainty, value investors care about long-term income uncertainty. The next chapter explains how that risk might be gauged.

References

Black, Fischer. 1972. Capital Market Equilibrium with Restricted Borrowing, *Journal of Business*, 45(3), 444–454.

Harvey, Campbell R., Liu, Yan, and Zhu, Heqing. 2016. … and the Cross-Section of Expected Returns, *Review of Financial Studies*, 29(10), 5–68.

Fama, Eugene F., and French, Kenneth R. 1993. Common Risk Factors in the Returns on Stocks and Bonds, *Journal of Financial Economics*, 33(1), 3–56.

Fama, Eugene F., and French, Kenneth R. 2004. The Capital Asset Pricing Model: Theory and Evidence, *Journal of Economic Perspectives*, 18(3), 25–46.

Fama, Eugene F., and French, Kenneth R. 2015. A Five-Factor Asset Pricing Model, *Journal of Financial Economics*, 116(1), 1–22.

Feng, Guanhao, Giglio, Stefano, and Xiu, Dacheng. 2020. Taming the Factor Zoo, *The Journal of Finance*, 75(3), 1327–1370.

Lintner, John. 1965. The Valuation of Risk Assets and the Selection of Risky Investments in Stock Portfolios and Capital Budgets, *Review of Economics and Statistics*, 47(1), 13–37.

Liu, Yukun, and Tsyvinski, Aleh. 2018. Risks and Returns of Cryptocurrency, NBER Working Paper No. 24877, August 13.

Merton, Robert C. 1973. An Intertemporal Capital Asset Pricing Model, *Econometrica*, 41(5), 867–887.

Sharpe, W. F. 1964. Capital Asset Prices: A Theory of Market Equilibrium Under Conditions of Risk, *The Journal of Finance*, 19(3), 425–442.

6

Investing 6.0—Modern Value Investing

Investing 1.0 consisted of little more than speculative guesses about whether stock prices were headed up or down. It was a fertile field for market manipulation and speculative bubbles and there were plenty of both. Pump-and-dump schemes were rampant (and legal!) and there was a seemingly endless supply of suckers and greater fools.

After the Roaring Twenties and the Great Crash, John Burr Williams and Benjamin Graham revolutionized stock analysis with the powerful Investing 2.0 (value-investing) argument that investors should stop trying to predict ups and downs in stock prices and, instead, focus on corporate assets, earnings, and dividends. The intrinsic value of a stock is the present value of its income, as measured, for example, by its dividends, free cash flow, and economic value added. To keep from being distracted by price predictions, value investors can assume that they will hold their stocks forever—which makes future prices irrelevant. However, this—the original value-investing approach—paid scant attention to the reality that stocks are risky because the future income from stocks is uncertain.

Investing 3.0 (mean–variance analysis) proposed using the standard deviation of short-term returns to measure the risk of investing in stocks. Since the volatility of short-term returns depends mainly on the volatility of stock prices, mean–variance analysis has the unfortunate consequence of redirecting attention away from the income received from stocks and back toward short-term price changes. In mean–variance analysis, stocks are considered risky if their prices fluctuate a lot.

Investing 4.0 introduced the efficient market hypothesis, which was often tested by using mean–variance analysis to assess the riskiness of various strategies, and again diverted attention away from intrinsic values and toward the short-term volatility of stock prices. The failure of actively managed mutual funds to beat the market, after taking into account short-term price volatility, led to the growth of index funds.

Investing 5.0 added CAPM, factor models, and algorithmic trading, all of which focus on short-term changes in stock prices. Taken together, mean–variance analysis, indexing, CAPM, factor models, and computer algos—are all value-agnostic strategies that ignore and undermine the insights of value investing. None of these strategies try to estimate intrinsic values, let alone compare intrinsic values to market prices.

The odd thing about this mindset is that if a company were privately held and had issued no publicly traded stock, potential buyers would not think about short-term fluctuations in the market value of the company. They would not assume that the asking price is the efficient market correct price. They would not use CAPM, factor models, or computer algorithms to tell them whether or not to buy the company. Potential buyers would focus on the same thing that value investors focus on for publicly traded corporations—the company's assets and profits.

Nor do the potential buyers of a private company use the standard deviation of short-term price fluctuations to gauge risk. Instead, they make projections of the company's long-run profitability and think seriously about how much confidence they have in their projections.

We believe that the time is ripe for a similar approach to assessing the real value and real risks of investing in stocks. A modern value-investing approach—Investing 6.0—returns to the insights of value investing and measures risk not by the short-term volatility of stock prices but by the uncertainty of the cash flow.

Mean–variance analysis, CAPM, and factor models make no attempt to explain *why* a stock's price might go up or down, *why* the price might fluctuate a little or a lot, or *why* there might be high or low correlations among stock prices. The approach is very much like Mr. Market drawing numbers out of a hat.

Without a structural model to explain price changes, investors must necessarily rely on historical means, standard deviations, and correlations and their efforts are severely undermined by the reality that past price fluctuations are an unreliable guide to future price fluctuations.

Value investors, in contrast, can use plausible forward-looking models to predict company revenue, expenses, profits, dividends, and other relevant financial data. The predictions are not infallible, but they provide a structural framework for gauging uncertainty. Value investors might consider plausible ranges for product demand, market share, costs, and so on because these are the relevant uncertainties for investors who are considering buying a privately held business and they are the relevant uncertainties for investors who are considering buying shares in a publicly traded company.

A Better Measure of Risk

A value-investing approach suggests that risk would be better measured by long-run uncertainty about the income from an asset than by short-run uncertainty about the price of the asset. Investors should look forward, not backward, and estimate the income from their investments *and* their uncertainty about those estimates.

For a simple example, we will use the JBW constant-dividend-growth equation that was discussed in Chapter 2 to show how risk over a long horizon can be assessed:

$$V = \frac{D}{R - g} \qquad (6.1)$$

John Burr Williams looked at future dividends and we will too, but, as noted earlier, we can also look at dividends plus share repurchases, free cash flow, or economic value added.

Let's use annual numbers and assume a $3 dividend, 8% required return, and 5% dividend growth rate. The intrinsic value is $100:

$$V = \frac{\$3}{0.08 - 0.05} = \$100$$

Which components of this equation are uncertain? Our required return R depends on the current interest rates on Treasury bonds, which are known when we are doing our valuation analysis. There is generally little uncertainty about the next dividend but considerable uncertainty about the growth rate of dividends. Thus, our uncertainty about the intrinsic value of a stock is mostly uncertainty about future dividends (or whichever alternative measure of cash flow we are using). In the JBW constant-dividend-growth model, uncertainty about future dividends is summarized by uncertainty about the value of the dividend growth rate g.

We might believe, for example, that the most likely long-run average dividend growth rate is 5% but that there is a 10% chance that the value will be 4% (or lower), which reduces the intrinsic value to $75 (or lower):

$$V = \frac{\$3}{0.08 - 0.04} = \$75$$

With this assumption, an investor who buys the stock for $75 believes that there is a 10% chance that they overpaid.

Notice that uncertainty for a value investor has nothing to do with fluctuations in the stock's price after the purchase has been made. As Warren Buffett once advised, "I buy on the assumption that they could close the market the next day and not reopen it for five years." For a value investor, the relevant uncertainty is whether the future income will be sufficient to justify the purchase price. It is exceedingly difficult to look at a stock and not notice what the price has been in the past and not think about what the price might be in the future but that's what value investors should try to do. As we said in Chapter 2, value investing requires discipline.

We can use a probability distribution for the dividend growth rate to provide a more sophisticated description of our uncertainty. To illustrate, consider the normal distribution shown in Fig. 6.1. The expected value of the growth rate is 5% and the standard deviation is 0.5%, Using the two standard deviations rule for normal distributions, the investor is 95% confident that the long-run growth rate will be between 4 and 6%. In addition, the investor can rule out extreme values by stating that the long-run growth rate has no chance of being below 3% or above 7%.

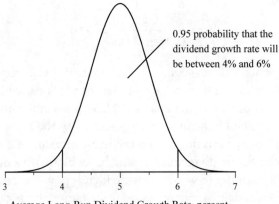

Fig. 6.1 Modeling uncertainty about future dividends

Notice, again, that we are describing our uncertainty about the future. We may use historical dividend data to inform our predictions but we do not naively assume that future dividends will be random draws from a hat filled with past dividend numbers.

Figure 6.2 shows the implied probability distribution for the intrinsic value V. (We used computer simulations to determine this distribution.) This probability distribution is skewed slightly to the right with a median of $100 and mean of $103. There is approximately a 7% probability that the value is less than $80, which we can interpret by saying that, if this investor can buy the stock for $80, they believe that there is only a 7% chance that they will have paid too much. This is a simple quantification of Graham's margin of safety (mentioned in Chapter 3).

Another way of describing our uncertainty is to calculate the value surplus VS, the percentage difference between the intrinsic value V and the market price P:

$$VS = 100\left(\frac{V-P}{P}\right) \qquad (6.2)$$

Value investors should be attracted to stocks with positive value surpluses—the larger the better. The advantage of working with the value surplus, rather than the dollar difference between intrinsic value and market price, is that it is a percentage metric. A $20 stock with a $30 intrinsic value is more attractive than a $200 stock with a $220 intrinsic value because the value surplus is 50% for the first stock, and only 10% for the second stock.

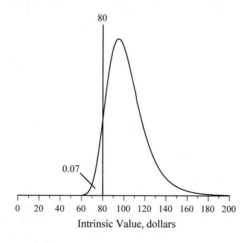

Fig. 6.2 Our uncertainty about a stock's intrinsic value

In the spring of 2023, a value investor we respect greatly estimated that Cisco had an intrinsic value of $55 and a market price of $45, while Honeywell had an intrinsic value of $195 and a market price of $180. Which stock had a larger value surplus? Even though Honeywell had a larger difference between intrinsic value and market price ($15 versus $10), Cisco had a higher value surplus:

$$\text{Cisco VS} = 100\left(\frac{\$55 - \$45}{\$45}\right) = 22.2\%$$

$$\text{Honeywell VS} = 100\left(\frac{\$195 - \$180}{\$180}\right) = 8.3\%$$

For the example shown earlier in Fig. 6.2, the probability distribution of the value surplus is shown in Fig. 6.3, with the percentage value surplus shown on the horizontal axis instead of the dollar intrinsic value. For a market price of $80, there is a 0.07 probability that the value surplus is negative. The probability distribution of the value surplus has a mean of 29% and a median of 24%.

The value surplus depends on both the intrinsic value V and the market price P. Specifically, if an investor buys a stock and the market price then falls, it is tempting to think that the stock was a bad investment and sell the stock before the price falls further. However, if the intrinsic value has not fallen (or fallen less than the price), the value surplus actually increases—making the stock *more* attractive. More generally, mean–variance analysis gauges risk by the volatility of stock prices. Value investors can embrace price fluctuations because they may create profitable buying and selling opportunities.

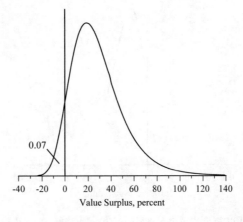

Fig. 6.3 Our uncertainty about a stock's value surplus

We reiterate this because the value surplus model is so different from conventional approaches to investing. The value surplus model follows John Burr Williams in not attempting to predict future stock prices, either in the short run or long run. The presumption is that buying an asset that is worth more to you than the price you paid is an attractive financial proposition.

In the mean–variance model and CAPM, risk is measured by the short-run volatility of prices and there is no attempt to explain *why* stock prices might be volatile. In the value surplus model, risk comes from the unpredictability of future cash flows and is measured by uncertainty about the value surplus—which can be assessed.

For a recent real-life example, consider Meta (formerly Facebook) at the end of 2021. The most relevant risk at that time was not that Meta had an above-average beta and the stock market might crash but that Meta's future cash flow might be jeopardized by competition, regulation, or other factors. As it turned out, Meta's income and earnings per share plummeted in 2022 and so did projections of its future growth. The intrinsic value of Meta collapsed and so did the stock price.

Consider, also, a large well-managed oil and natural gas company like Exxon. The biggest risk for long-term investors is not that the daily stock price will dance wildly but that there will be a long-term decline in oil and natural gas prices because of the development of more efficient technology or a shift toward alternative energy sources. The fundamental uncertainty is not about short-term swings in investors' moods but long-run trends in the market for the company's products. The same can be said for most companies. Investors thinking about buying Apple, Google, Starbucks, Home Depot, or Netflix should think about the source of the company's profits and possible long-term threats to those profits, not the standard deviation of the company's daily stock price over the past few years.

Diversification with a Value Surplus Approach

It is tempting to evaluate stocks one by one, buying those with the most favorable value surpluses. However, the risk of paying too much can be reduced by purchasing several stocks with (1) attractive value surpluses, and (2) dividend growth rates that are lightly correlated or uncorrelated. Figure 6.4 compares the distribution of the value surplus for the single stock in Fig. 6.3 with the value surplus for a 50–50 investment in this stock and

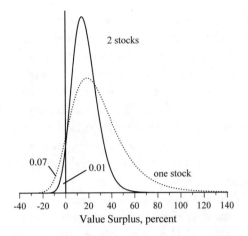

Fig. 6.4 A 50–50 investment in two stocks with uncorrelated growth rates reduces risk

an identical stock with an uncorrelated dividend growth rate. Diversification does not affect the average value of the value surplus, but reduces the probability that the portfolio's value surplus is negative from 0.07 to 0.01.

We can also show (but won't here) that the amount of risk reduction depends on the correlation between the two dividend growth rates. The lower the correlation, the less likely it is that the portfolio value surplus is negative. The important distinction is that when a value investor looks to diversify, the relevant question is not whether short-term price fluctuations are correlated but whether long-term cash flows are.

We can also construct a value-investing mean–variance graph like Fig. 3.3 in Chapter 3. The crucial difference is that standard portfolio theory looks at the means and standard deviations of short-term returns, while a value investor looks at the means and standard deviations of the value surplus. Figure 6.5 gives an example of the two stocks summarized in Table 6.1.

The black dots labeled "1" and "2" are the means and standard deviations of the value surplus for 100% investments in either stock. The curved line shows how the standard deviation of the value surplus is reduced by investing in both stocks. It is noteworthy that many portfolios have less risk than does either stock individually. The portfolio with the lowest standard deviation consists of 38% Stock 1 and 62% Stock 2.

Figure 6.5 follows modern portfolio theory in using the standard deviation to gauge risk. A reasonable alternative is shown in Fig. 6.6, which gauges risk by the probability that the portfolio value surplus is negative. Notice that although Stock 1's value surplus has a higher standard deviation, the mean is sufficiently high to give it a lower probability of a negative value surplus.

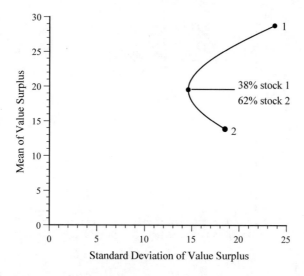

Fig. 6.5 A mean-standard deviation tradeoff for a portfolio's value surplus

Table 6.1 Assumed stock parameters used in Fig. 6.5

	Stock 1	Stock 2
Dividend D	3	5
Mean dividend growth rate g	0.05	0.03
Standard deviation of g	0.005	0.008
Minimum value of g	0.03	0.01
Maximum value of g	0.07	0.05
Correlation between the two growth rates	0.00	0.00
Required return R	0.08	0.08
Market price P	80	90
Mean of value surplus VS	28.79	13.87
Standard deviation of VS	23.68	18.49

This is a concrete example of how the standard deviation can be a misleading measure of the risks that matter to investors. If a value surplus has a high probability of being far above its expected value, this increases the standard deviation but also increases the chances of a favorable outcome.

Using the probability of a negative value surplus to gauge risk, the minimum-risk portfolio is 64% Stock 1 and 36% Stock 2. It is striking that the minimum standard deviation portfolio invests 62% in Stock 2 while the minimum-probability portfolio invests 64% in Stock 1. This is a concrete example of how the standard deviation is not an unambiguously superior measure of risk.

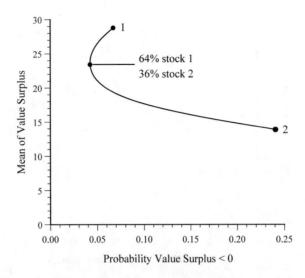

Fig. 6.6 A Mean-probability tradeoff for a portfolio's value surplus

Implications of a Value Surplus Approach

Value investors do not attempt to predict whether a stock's price is about to go up or down. Instead, they estimate the intrinsic value of a stock by discounting the projected cash flow over an essentially infinite horizon. The uncertainty in their analysis comes from their imperfect predictions of future cash flows rather than the unpredictability of near-term price fluctuations.

A forward-looking specification of probability distributions for the cash flow can be used to determine probability distributions for intrinsic values and value surpluses. A negative value surplus means that the market price is higher than the intrinsic value. Therefore, a compelling measure of risk is the probability that the value surplus is negative. If uncertainties about the cash flow from multiple investments are linked together through multivariate probability distributions (analogous to the covariances in mean–variance analysis), then the risk associated with alternative asset portfolios can be assessed by the probability that the portfolio value surplus is negative.

Value investors are naturally drawn to companies with a stable cash flow; for example, public utilities (like NRG Energy), conglomerates (like Unilever), or dominant brands (like Coca-Cola). The ideal stock would be one that has a reliable cash flow and a market price substantially below intrinsic value. Value investors welcome price volatility because it allows for tax harvesting and advantageous trades.

Mean–variance analysis and the capital asset pricing model have been justifiably celebrated for their elegant mathematics and compelling insights, including the value of diversification and the importance of correlations among asset returns. However, they are value-agnostic strategies that ignore and undermine the insights of value investing. Even worse, they gauge risk by short-term fluctuations in market prices.

This misplaced focus not only distorts the choice of individual stocks, but it also warps the allocation of investments between stocks and bonds.

A Prevent Defense Is Seldom a Good Investment Strategy

American football coaches are notorious for putting their teams in "prevent-defense" mode when they have a small lead at the end of the game and want to prevent the other team from scoring a winning field goal or touchdown. For example, a team might have a 6-point lead with a minute left in the game and the other team on its own 20-yard line, 80 yards from scoring a winning touchdown. A prevent-defense strategy would use 5, 6, or even 7 defensive backs to guard against long passes.

It sometimes works. Often it doesn't, as the other team completes a rapid sequence of short passes (or even running plays) and wins the game. Cynics say that the only thing a prevent defense prevents is winning the game.

A lot of modern investment strategies remind us of the prevent defense—seemingly safe in the short run but costly in the long run. For instance, the 60/40 portfolio has long been considered a prudent strategy that balances the potential price appreciation from stocks with the relative stability of bond prices. Chapter 3 showed how this strategy can, in fact, hobble long-run portfolio returns because too much money is invested in low-return bonds in order to reduce short-run price volatility that many investors should not care about.

Target-date and age-in-bonds strategies are similarly motivated and similarly flawed. A target-date strategy selects a target retirement date and shifts from stocks to bonds as that date nears. For example, the default investment option for the retirement plan offered by Gary's employer is a Vanguard target fund that invests 90% in equities and 10% fixed income until the investor is 40 years old, then shifts gradually to 30% equites and 70% fixed income over the next 30 years, and stays at 30/70 after that. An age-in-bonds strategy is what it sounds like: 40% bonds for a 40-year-old, 60% bonds for a 60-year-old.

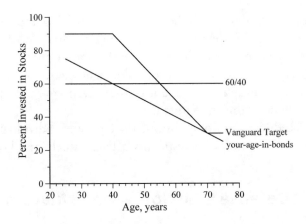

Fig. 6.7 Target, age, and 60/40 strategies

Figure 6.7 shows the percentage invested in stocks at various ages for the Vanguard Target Fund and an age-in-bonds plan. The average stock percentage is 66% for the Target strategy and 50% for the Age strategy.

As with the 60/40 rule, the motivation for these strategies is to reap the higher returns from stocks while using bonds to cushion short-term volatility. However, damping down short-term volatility is like a prevent defense in football—seeking short-run safety and sacrificing long-run success.

Leave Your Options Open

Prevent-defense investing reminds us of an argument we once heard about why women in less-developed countries have so many babies. An economist with a Ph.D. from MIT said that most families in these countries believe that it is very important that they have at least one son. If girl and boy babies are equally likely, no matter the sex of other children in the family, then it can be shown that a woman will need to have seven babies in order to be 99% sure of having at least one son. Are you persuaded by this argument?

It is true that if one has to commit to a fixed number of children before the first child is born, a mother will have to choose seven children to be 99% certain that at least one of her children will be a boy. However, the seven children will not be born all at once. The family can decide whether to have more children *after* seeing the children that have already been born. If the first child is a boy, the family can stop then; they are not required to have six more children.

Suppose that it is true that all any of the parents care about is having one son—so they will have children until a son is born, and then stop. Half the families will have one child, a boy. A quarter of the families will have two children, a girl and then a boy. An eighth of the families will have three children, two girls and then a boy. It can be shown mathematically that the average family size is two, not seven. Not only that but, since every family has exactly 1 boy, the total number of girls is equal to the total number of boys—which makes sense if girl and boy babies are equally likely.

In the same way, it doesn't make sense to commit to an extremely conservative investment strategy for the remainder of your life based on the possibility that the stock market might go down at some point. It makes more sense to invest with the expectation of making good returns and then shifting to a more conservative strategy if falling stock prices become a problem.

Details, Details

Target-return and your-age-in-bonds strategies wrongly assume that one strategy fits all. We disagree. A well-informed plan clearly depends on individual circumstances. Someone who never plans to retire is in a very different situation from someone who retires at 50. People who have paid off their home mortgages are in a different situation from people who rent or are still making mortgage payments. Some people live in New York City; others live in Indianapolis. Some people have built up large stock portfolios that generate substantial dividend income; others have virtually no retirement savings.

In addition, many people plan to make a substantial bequest to their relatives, alma mater, place of worship, or preferred charity. Planned bequests provide a cushion for their spending and wealth. If their investments do well, the bequests will be larger than they had planned. If their investments do poorly, they have the option of cutting back spending or trimming bequests. Choosing to make "safe" low-return investments is seldom the best choice.

We have a 50-year-old relative whose salary more than covers living expenses, expects to work for many more years, is earning substantial income from a stock portfolio, and will receive Social Security benefits at some point. A 50%-bond portfolio is likely to reduce the eventual bequest substantially and to make it more likely, not less likely, that this person will outlive their wealth. As time passes and this person becomes 60, 70, or 80 years old and switches to 60%, 70%, and 80% bonds, the costs will be even higher. If there is no imminent need to sell stocks, there is no need to hold large amounts of cash or low-interest bonds—let alone to hold more as one gets older.

There are, of course, situations in which an all-stock portfolio is genuinely risky—for example when cash is needed in sixty days to make a down payment on a house—but a universal 60/40, target retirement, or age-in-bonds strategy is surely a bad idea for many, if not most, people.

Let's see how such strategies have fared historically. The current age at which required minimum distributions (RMDs) from retirement plans must begin is 73. It is likely to go even higher in the future as life expectancies increase. We considered a monthly investment in stocks and bonds in a retirement fund, beginning at age 25 and continuing for up to 50 years, until age 75. We assumed that the monthly investment is initially $100 and grows by 5% annually but the results are easily scalable.

We looked at all possible starting dates in the historical data, as far back as the data go, to January 1926, a few years before the Great Crash. For stocks, the worst possible starting date was September 1929, but, even then, the initial $100 would have grown to $3190 after 50 years, which is a 7.2% annual return. The best month to start a 50-year stock market investment was July 1949; $100 would have grown to $68,740, which is a 14.0% annual return. The average 50-year return was 11.2%. For Treasury bonds, in contrast, the 50-year returns ranged from 2.5 to 8.4%, with an average of 5.9% ($100 growing to $1771). Yes, the worst stock market outcome ($3190) was 80% better than the average bond outcome ($1771).

The disappointing historical performance of bonds has been a drag on prevent-defense portfolio strategies. Figure 6.8 shows how often a 100% stock strategy did better than a prevent-defense strategy for our monthly saver over horizons ranging from one month to 50 years. Over 30-year horizons, the all-stocks strategy beat the target-return, age-in-bonds, and 60/40 strategies 88, 92, and 93% of the time, respectively. Over the 50-year horizons, stocks won 93, 98, and 99% of the time. The longer the horizon, the more certain it is that all stocks have been a winning strategy.

How much did it matter? A lot. Figure 6.9 shows the average wealth for our monthly saver over various horizons up to 50 years. The all-stocks strategy wound up with an average of $4.13 million after 50 years, compared to $2.67 million for the most successful prevent-defense strategy.

The past is no guarantee of the future. Indeed, the whole point of a value-investing perspective is to think about the future, not the past. When we compare stocks with bonds, looking forward instead of backward, stocks often look like a better long-run investment—just as they have been in the past.

In February 2023, we did just that. The yield on 30-year Treasury bonds was 3.75% and the dividends plus buybacks yield on the S&P 500 was

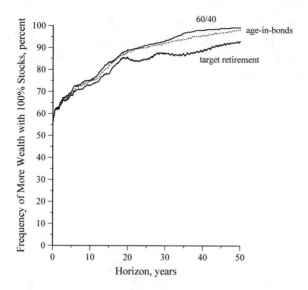

Fig. 6.8 Prevent-defense investment strategies usually lose the race

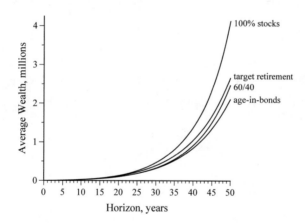

Fig. 6.9 An all-stocks strategy has trounced prevent-defense strategies

4.47%. If dividends plus buybacks were to increase over time, as they surely will, the long-run return from stocks would be higher—perhaps substantially higher—than 4.47%. With 5% growth in the economy and corporate disbursements, the long-run return from stocks will be close to double digits, as it has been in the past.

For long-term investors who can largely ignore short-term price volatility (or even profit from it with tax harvesting and advantageous transactions), it is hard to see how a prevent-defense investment strategy prevents anything other than victory.

A more compelling strategy is an Investing 6.0 value surplus approach with the attractiveness of stocks measured by their value surplus and risk measured by uncertainty about the future cash flow from investments.

The next chapter will analyze a specific case study.

7

A Case Study—Stocks

In this chapter, we will illustrate the Investing 6.0 value-surplus approach to choosing stocks by working though the details of a potential investment in Apple and JPMorgan Chase on January 17, 2023.

Apple is, of course, Apple with its iPhone, iPad, iMac, and iMore universe of loyal customers. As we write this in 2023, Apple has been the number one stock on *Fortune*'s annual list of the world's most-admired companies for 16 years in a row. It is hardly news when Apple is Number One; instead, it will be news when Apple is not Number One. Apple is the epitome of a cash cow. Over the past three years, its average return on assets was 20% and its average return on shareholder equity was 93%. Its cash hoard and sustained profitability bode well for future dividends and share repurchases.

JPMorgan Chase is a diversified financial powerhouse. (For simplicity, we will just refer to the company by its ticker symbol, JPM.) Measured by assets, JPM is the largest bank in the United States and the fifth largest bank in the world. Measured by market value, it is the largest bank in the world. JPM's profits are immense, but volatile, because, like all banks, it borrows from some in order to lend to others and is consequently highly leveraged. Consider this highly condensed bank balance sheet:

Assets (billions)		Liabilities (billions)	
Cash	$4	Deposits	$90
Loans	$96	Net Worth	$10
Total	$100	Total	$100

© The Author(s), under exclusive license to Springer Nature Switzerland AG 2023
G. Smith and M. Smith, *The Power of Modern Value Investing*,
https://doi.org/10.1007/978-3-031-45900-9_7

This hypothetical bank has 10-to-1 leverage in that its total assets are 10 times the size of its net worth, which means that a 1% change in the value of its assets will cause a 10% change in its net worth. Suppose, for example, that $2 billion of its loans default. That's a 2% drop in assets but the bank's net worth will drop by 20%, from $10 billion to $8 billion.

Assets (billions)		Liabilities (billions)	
Cash	$4	Deposits	$90
Loans	$94	Net Worth	$8
Total	$98	Total	$98

It is not just loan defaults that have magnified effects on net worth. So, too, do changes in the bank's income and expenses and changes in the market value of its assets and liabilities.

JPM manages these risks well, but these risks are large and very different risks from those faced by Apple. In *Fortune*'s annual most-admired list, JPM had been among the top 10 in each of the past five years. We chose these two companies because of their stellar reputations and because they are in quite different industries.

An Investing 1.0 Approach

An Investing 1.0 approach would focus on trying to predict which direction these two stock prices will go next. Technical analysts might examine a price chart like that shown in Fig. 7.1 for JPM. Along with the daily prices, this chart shows two moving averages—the average price over the previous 50 days and the average price over the previous 200 days. When the 50-day moving average crosses and goes above the 200-day average, this is called a *golden cross* and is a very bullish signal for technical analysts. When, as in Fig. 7.1, the 50-day average crosses and goes below the 200-day average, this is called a *death cross* and is very bearish. Unfortunately, neither predictor works reliably. Nor do other predictors of short-term changes in stock prices.

A value-investing approach is quite different but we will postpone our discussion of how value investors might evaluate Apple and JPM until we cover the other alternative approaches that have been used over time.

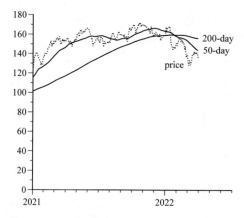

Fig. 7.1 JPM's stock price and two moving averages

An Investing 3.0 Approach

The Investing 3.0 approach is mean–variance analysis (aka modern portfolio theory). A mean–variance investor who restricted his or her attention to these two stocks might use historical data to estimate the means and standard deviations of the historical returns and the correlation between these two stock returns. The University of Pennsylvania's Wharton Research Data Services (WRDS) provides a wealth of data for analyzing stocks and we often turn to it to find accurate historical data. WRDS also has a product, called "Efficient Frontier," which calculates the historical means, standard deviations, and correlations and "the corresponding Efficient Frontier…[and] Minimum Variance Portfolio." Using monthly data back to 2012, the program reported the frontier shown in Fig. 7.2 with the minimum-risk portfolio being 40% Apple and 60% JPM. An investor who is willing to tolerate more risk might hold more than 40% Apple.

The critical problem with this approach is that past means, standard deviations, and correlations are an unreliable guide to future performance. Value investors also dismiss this approach because it gauges risk by short-term price jiggles that are large irrelevant to a value analysis.

The Collapse of SVB

The 2023 bankruptcy of the nation's 16th largest bank, Silicon Valley Bank (SVB), is a good example of the difference between short-run stock price fluctuations and the real risks banks face. SVB had long been an integral part

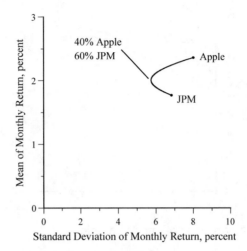

Fig. 7.2 The WRDS efficient frontier

of the Silicon Valley startup scene, lending money to venture-capital-backed companies and holding their operating cash as bank deposits. An obvious risk is that borrowers will go bust and not repay their loans.

A not-so-obvious risk is that SVB used short-term deposits to finance a substantial investment in long-term bonds—and when interest rates go up, bond prices go down. So, SVB was making a risky wager that interest rates wouldn't go up much.

Unfortunately for SVB, the rate of inflation rose from 1.4% in 2021 to 7.5% in 2022 and the Federal Reserve started raising interest rates in the spring of 2022 to slow inflation. As interest rates went up, the market value of SVB's long-term bonds went down. They were able to maintain a temporary illusion of solvency by valuing most of their bonds at face value rather than market value but savvy Silicon Valley depositors saw through this accounting trick and, knowing that their deposits were only insured up to $250,000, withdrew tens of billions of dollars. To satisfy these withdrawals, SVB was forced to sell some of its bonds for a $1.8 billion loss. The next domino was nervous investors fleeing SVB stock, which fell 60% on Thursday, March 9, 2023, and then fell another 65% by the time markets opened Friday. Before the day was over, the FDIC had closed SVB.

Well-managed banks, like JPM, try to protect their balance sheets from fluctuations in interest rates. SVB did not—though it is unclear whether this was out of arrogance or ignorance. Our point is that the real risk for those who invested in SVB stock was not the standard deviation of daily fluctuations in its stock price but by the possibility that many of the startups it financed would fail and by the possibility that interest rates would increase substantially.

An Investing 4.0 Approach

In contrast to an Investing 3.0 approach that uses historical data to construct mean–variance portfolios, the Investing 4.0 approach ignores the past completely because it assumes that the stock market is efficient and that all stocks are priced correctly, including Apple at $135/share and JPM at $143/share on January 17, 2023, when we did this analysis. Seeking diversification, an efficient market believer might invest in an S&P 500 index fund that holds modest amounts of Apple and JPM.

The S&P 500 weights stocks by their market values. On January 17, 2023, Apple was the most valuable company in the S&P 500, with a market value equal to 6.02% of the total value of all stocks in the S&P 500. JPM was the 11th largest company, with a weight of 1.25%. An indexer would hold nearly 5 times as much Apple as JPM, but both stocks would be a very small part of their portfolio.

Value investors, in contrast, believe that Mr. Market often sets stock prices far higher or lower than intrinsic values. They would not hold five times as much Apple as JPM simply because Apple's market value is five times that of JPM, nor would they hold small amounts of each stock simply because there are lots of other stocks in the S&P 500.

An Investing 5.0 Approach

Investing 5.0 involves CAPM, multiple-factor models, and algorithmic trading. Figures 7.3 and 7.4 show the estimates of the beta coefficients for Apple and JPM using five years of monthly stock returns in the WRDS database. Since Apple's beta is 1.21 and JMP's beta is 1.13, a CAPM enthusiast would conclude that Apple is slightly riskier than JPM and that both are riskier than the market as a whole.

Since the two beta coefficients are approximately equal, there is no compelling reason to hold more of one stock than the other. Those who do not want a portfolio that is riskier than the S&P 500 would have little reason to invest much in either stock. Value investors ignore beta coefficients because

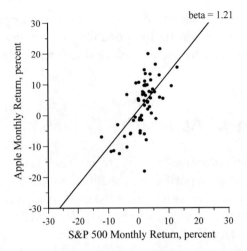

Fig. 7.3 Apple's beta coefficient

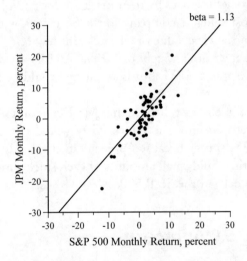

Fig. 7.4 JPM's beta coefficient

they relate to short-term price movements (and, even worse, are based on past price movements).

Models with multiple factors might consider correlations of Apple and JPM stock prices with literally any economic variable. We are not going to bother doing that. Algorithmic models cast the net wider, even looking at social media data, and might conclude that Apple stock does well after there is a surge in Google searches for the word *Neymar* and that JPM does well after an uptick in Elon Musk tweets that include the word *bird*. (These are hypothetical but typical examples.) We are not going to go there either.

A Modern Value-Investing Approach

Instead, we will discuss how a value investor might evaluate Apple and JPM stock. The intrinsic value of a stock is what an investor who has no intention of ever selling would pay to receive all the cash generated by the stock. We will use the John Burr Williams constant-growth equation that was introduced in Chapter 2 and use real, inflation-adjusted values for the model's variables:

$$V = \frac{D}{R - g}$$

Williams just considered the dividends paid to stockholders because, at the time, share repurchases were rare. However, the cash returned to stockholders includes both dividends and share repurchases. The simplest way to see this is to imagine that there is only a single person who owns all of Apple's stock and receives all of the cash that Apple pays out in dividends and share repurchases. The intrinsic value of all of Apple's stock is clearly the value of both the dividends and the share repurchases. The value of a single share is equal to the total value divided by the number of shares outstanding, and includes both dividends and repurchases.

This logic is important for analyzing Apple because, as Fig. 7.5 shows, it has recently been giving far more cash to shareholders though repurchases than through dividends—which is a wise move because, as explained in Chapter 2, stock buybacks are better than dividends from a tax perspective. In the fiscal year ending on September 30, 2022, Apple distributed a total of $14.8 billion in dividends and $89.4 billion in repurchases ($0.91/share versus $6.38/share).

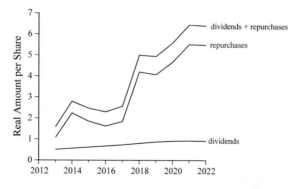

Fig. 7.5 Apple's share repurchases are much larger than its dividends

Figure 7.6 shows that over the previous 10 years, Apple's real, inflation-adjusted sum of dividends plus repurchases has grown at an annual rate of 17% a year. That is clearly not sustainable, so we will calculate an extremely conservative valuation using the constant-growth model with a long-run 2% average real growth rate. This is somewhat lower than the 3% average annual growth rate of U.S. real GDP since 1950 and roughly equal to long-run projections for the U.S. economy. Apple is not an average company, but we want to be conservative and the long run is, well, the long run.

JPM's real shareholder income has also increased at a 17% rate over the preceding 10 years, but Fig. 7.7 shows that there has been considerably more year-to-year variation than has been true of Apple. We will also assume a long-run 2% average real growth rate for JPM.

We used the fitted lines in Figs. 7.6 and 7.7 to project the 2023 shareholder income for each company—$7.00 for Apple and $9.28 for JPM.

Now, we have values of D and g in the constant-growth valuation equation but we still need a value for R, our required real rate of return. Writing in January 2023, the real yield on 30-year Treasury Inflation Protected Securities (TIPS) was 1.44%. We will use a 6% real required return for Apple and a 7% required return for JPM since there seems to be more uncertainty about its income. (You should use your own personal inflation-adjusted

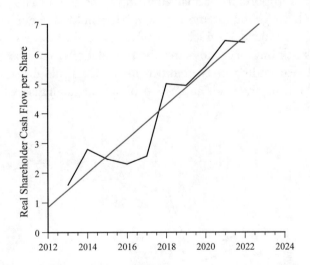

Fig. 7.6 Apple's shareholder income, 2013–2023

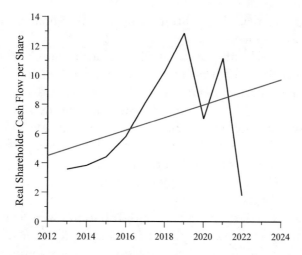

Fig. 7.7 JPM's shareholder income, 2013–2023

required returns.) With these assumptions, Apple and JPM's intrinsic values are comfortably above their respective market prices at the time, $135 and $143:

$$\text{Apple}: V = \frac{\$7.00}{0.06 - 0.02} = \$175$$

$$\text{JPM}: V = \frac{\$9.28}{0.07 - 0.02} = \$186$$

Oddly enough, the value surplus for each stock is 30%:

$$\text{Apple}: VS = 100\frac{\$175 - \$135}{\$135} = 30\%$$

$$\text{JPM}: VS = 100\frac{\$186 - \$143}{\$143} = 30\%$$

Gauging Uncertainty

To deal with the uncertainty in these valuations, consider the fact that the required return in the John Burr Williams model depends on current interest rates, and these are known at the time of the valuation. The main uncertainty is the long-run growth rate of dividends plus repurchases. Our perception in

January 2023 was that JPM's future income to shareholders is less certain than Apple's future income.

Working with real, inflation-adjusted data, an investor might summarize his or her uncertainty about the growth rate of Apple's dividends plus repurchases by using a normal distribution with a mean of 2% and a standard deviation of 0.5%. This assumption implies that the investor believes with 95% certainty that Apple's long-run inflation-adjusted growth rate is between 1% and 3%. We can use these assumptions to determine a probability distribution for Apple's value surplus. Figure 7.8 shows that, with our assumptions, there is only a 1% chance that Apple's value surplus is negative (that is, that its intrinsic value is less than $135.

For JPM, we will again use a normal distribution for its long-run growth rate but this time with a mean of 2% and a standard deviation of 1.0% (twice the standard deviation for Apple). A 1% standard deviation implies that we believe with 95% certainty that JPM's long-run inflation-adjusted growth rate is between 0% and 4%. Figure 7.9 shows that, with these assumptions, there is a 7% probability that JPM's value surplus is negative.

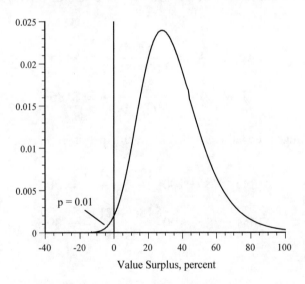

Fig. 7.8 Uncertainty about the intrinsic value of Apple

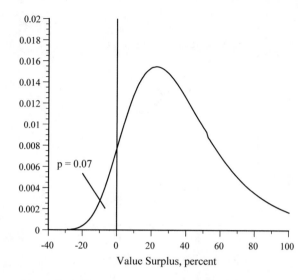

Fig. 7.9 Uncertainty about the intrinsic value of JPM

An Efficient Frontier

We can also take an intrinsic value approach to constructing a portfolio of stocks. Here, we consider just two stocks, Apple and JPM, but the analysis can be extended to any number of candidates.

We assumed a 0.2 correlation between Apple and JPM's long-run growth rates—if our estimate of Apple's growth rate turns out to be too high, then our estimate of JPM's growth rate will probably be too high, too. We believe these growth rates are positively correlated because both depend on the long-run growth rates of the United States and world economies. However, we also believe that the correlation is not strong because Apple and JPM are in very different industries.

Using this assumption, Fig. 7.10 shows the means and standard deviations of portfolios containing various combinations of Apple and JPM. The point labeled "JPM" is a 100% investment in JPM; the point labeled "Apple" is a 100% investment in Apple. The curved line running between these two extremes shows the means and standard deviations for various combinations of JPM and Apple.

It is interesting to compare this value-surplus frontier with the mean–variance frontier shown in Fig. 7.5 earlier in this chapter. The traditional mean–variance frontier is based on backward-looking historical price changes and says that the minimum-risk portfolio is 40% Apple and 60% JPM. The

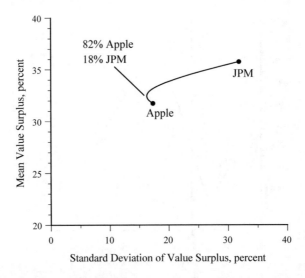

Fig. 7.10 The value-surplus mean-standard deviation frontier for Apple and JPM

value-surplus frontier in Fig. 7.10 is based on forward-looking income projections and identifies the minimum-risk portfolio as being very different: 82% Apple and 18% JPM.

The standard deviation is not necessarily the most relevant measure of risk. An attractive value-investing alternative is the probability that the portfolio's value surplus is negative—in which case, the stocks cost more than they are worth. Figure 7.11 shows the available combinations of the mean value-surplus and the probability that the value surplus is negative. The minimum-risk portfolio is 74% Apple and 26% JPM. The intrinsic value analysis in Figs. 7.10 and 7.11 gives slightly different results, but these results are quite different from the standard mean–variance analysis based on historical fluctuations in stock prices.

A modern value-investing approach is very different from alternatives such as speculation, mean–variance analysis, CAPM, factor models, and algos. Instead of using short-term price gyrations to predict returns and measure risk, modern value investing focuses investor attention on what really matters most—the long-term income from our investments and the confidence we have in those predictions.

It should not be surprising that, as in this Apple/JPM example, the conclusions can be quite dissimilar. Past price fluctuations and future income projections are fundamentally different information and will often lead to contrasting recommendations.

7 A Case Study—Stocks

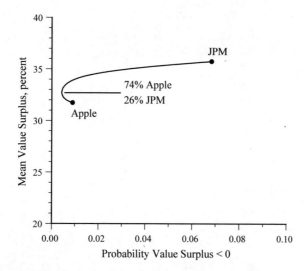

Fig. 7.11 The mean-probability frontier for Apple and JPM

8

A Case Study—Homes

In this chapter, we apply the Investing 6.0 value-surplus approach to buying a residential home, one of our favorite investments. In 2005 the Brookings Institution commissioned us to do a study of what many considered at the time to be a nationwide housing bubble. The evidence of a bubble was mainly that home prices had been increasing rapidly:

1. Home prices had increased faster than the consumer price index.
2. Home prices had increased faster than GDP.
3. Home prices had increased faster than construction costs.

Many home price indexes track the average sale price. The problem with such indexes is that the homes may not be comparable. The homes sold in 2004 might happen to be larger or to be in nicer locations than the homes that were sold in 2003. If so, the average sale price might go up in 2004 even though the prices of comparable homes actually fell.

The Federal Housing Finance Agency (FHFA) handles this problem by comparing the prices of homes that have been sold more than once during the period being studied. If, for example, a home was sold in 1990 for $300,000 and sold again in 2000 for $400,000, this would represent a 2.92% annual rate of increase over this 10-year period. Using data for all repeat sales, the FHFA calculates a Home Price Index (HPI) that best summarizes all of the observed price increases during the period being studied.

Figure 8.1 confirms that, starting around 1986, the HPI started increasing faster than the consumer price index (CPI) and that this gap exploded after 1999. It seemed clear that a housing bubble was forming.

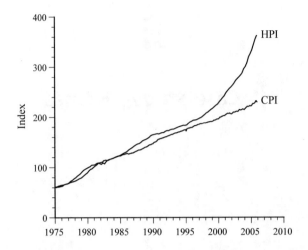

Fig. 8.1 The U.S. home price index (HPI) and consumer price index (CPI)

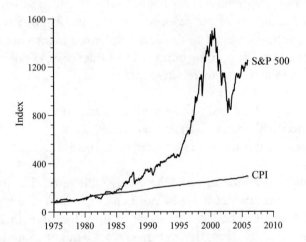

Fig. 8.2 A stock market bubble?

On the other hand, Fig. 8.2 shows that the S&P 500 index of stock prices had risen even faster than the HPI relative to the consumer price index. There was a dot-com bubble in the late 1990s and a subsequent crash but, even after the crash, stock prices far outpaced consumer prices. Were we still in a stock market bubble that started in 1985?

There is no particular reason why home prices or stock prices should increase at the same rate as consumer prices, so such comparisons are not a reliable sign of a bubble. An alternative measure is a comparison of home prices with GDP, since household income affects how much people can afford to spend on housing. However, affordability also depends on interest rates.

When mortgage rates drop, monthly mortgage payments fall, too, and people with the same income can afford to buy more expensive homes. More fundamentally, affordability is not a direct measure of a bubble. As we write this in June 2023, Berkshire Hathaway stock sells for more than $500,000 a share. This stock is not affordable for most people but that doesn't mean there is a Berkshire bubble.

Another possible measure of froth is a comparison of housing prices with construction costs. Home prices are affected by construction costs because builders will charge more for houses if it costs more to build houses. On the other hand, when people are looking to buy a house, the three most important considerations are location, location, location. In many places, the price of a home depends more on its location than on construction costs and location value may well increase faster than construction costs.

Recognizing Bubbles

Using this reasoning, we did not look at the simple bubble benchmarks that others were touting. Instead, we used intrinsic value principles. The way to determine whether there is a stock market bubble is to calculate the present value of the anticipated income from the stocks in, say, the S&P 500 and then compare this intrinsic value to the market price of the S&P 500. That is exactly what we did in earlier chapters.

A dramatic example happened on March 11, 2000, when Gary was one of four speakers at a March 11, 2000, conference on the "Dow 36K," a fashionable theory that the Dow Jones Industrial Average should be three times its level of around 12,000. After the three other speakers at this conference endorsed the 36K theory enthusiastically, Gary gave a contrarian view, ending with the warning, "This is a bubble, and it will end badly."

In Chapter 3, we recounted Zvi Bodie's apocalyptic warning in March 2009: "Unless you have the heart of a high stakes gambler, get out of stocks now." A few months earlier, in a December 2008 television interview, Gary had said precisely the opposite, "This is a buying opportunity that only comes around a half dozen times in a lifetime."

Figure 8.3 shows that both of Gary's assessments were correct.

Why did Gary believe there was a bubble in 2000 and an irresistible buying opportunity in December 2008? He compared the level of the S&P 500 with his estimate of the intrinsic value of the stocks in the S&P 500. We did the same in our Brookings study. We compared the prices of homes to our estimates of their intrinsic value.

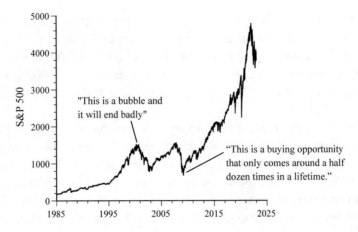

Fig. 8.3 Using intrinsic value estimates to assess the stock market

The Intrinsic Value of Homes

What is the income from a home that is analogous to the dividends from stock? If you buy a home and rent it to someone else, the income is the rent you receive (net of expenses). If you live in the house you bought, the implicit income is the money you save by not having to pay rent to live in the house.

Thus, the intrinsic value of an owner-occupied home is the present value of the rent savings net of other expenses like home insurance, property taxes, mortgage payments, and maintenance. To make clear the analogy to stocks, we called this net income the "home dividend."

At the time there was no Zillow (it was founded in 2006) so we gathered our housing data from the Multiple Listing Service (MLS) database. Neither of us had the real estate license needed to gain access to MLS data but we found realtors in 10 metropolitan areas that shared MLS data with us: Atlanta, Boston, Chicago, Dallas, Indianapolis, Los Angeles County, New Orleans, Orange County, San Bernardino County, and San Mateo County.

In each area, we scoured the MLS database looking for rents and prices of comparable single-family homes. Occasionally, we found a house that had been rented and was then sold, or a house that was purchased and then rented. Other times, we found essentially adjacent tract homes that had been built within a year of each other and had exactly the same number of bedrooms and bathrooms and square feet—with one house rented and the other sold recently. More often, we found close, but not perfect, matches.

Our matching criteria was that the rental and sale properties could differ by no more than 100 square feet in size, no more than 1 bedroom, and no more than half a bath. When the information was available, we also compared the houses' ages, style (for example, 1-story), and amenities (such as a pool and the size of the garage). Yahoo maps was used to estimate the driving distance between properties (no more than 1 mile) and to identify golf courses, parks, lakes, major highways, and other physical objects that might add to or detract from a house's value. It was evident from these maps that driving distance often exaggerates the physical distance between houses; for example, two houses might have adjoining back yards but have a driving distance of 0.1 or even 0.2 miles.

In addition to the rent savings, we assumed a 20% down payment, 30-year mortgage, 5.7% mortgage rate (the average 30-year mortgage rate in mid-July 2005), buyer's closing costs equal to 0.5% of the sale price, annual maintenance equal to 1% of the price, and a 28% federal income tax rate for those who deduct the property taxes and mortgage interest from their taxable income. State and metropolitan-area data were used for property taxes, state income taxes, and home insurance. Our baseline model assumed a 3% annual increase in housing rents and expenses (roughly the historical and predicted rate of CPI inflation at the time). We had presented some preliminary calculations at a meeting of 27 Certified Financial Planners (CFPs) and asked them what required after-tax return they would use if they adopted our house-valuation methodology; all answered either 5% or 6%. We used 6% to be conservative.

Our results confirmed the wisdom of the adage that all real estate is local. It is misleading to speak of homes in general as being cheap or expensive or there being a nationwide housing bubble. It really is all about location, location, location. The median value surplus for the homes we looked ranged from negative 35% (bubbly) in San Mateo to 186% (a very hot deal) in Indianapolis.

A Home in Fishers, Indiana

One of our examples is a 3-bedroom, 3-bathroom, 1917 square-foot home in Fishers, Indiana, a suburb of Indianapolis. At the time of our study, Fishers had a population of about 50,000 with a median family income of around $100,000. *Money* magazine ranked Fishers as among the top 50 places to live in the United States in 2005, and has continued to rank Fishers among the top 50 places multiple times. In 2017, Fishers was rated #1 in the country; in 2019, it was rated #3.

This home in Fishers was purchased for $135,000 on April 27, 2005, and rented for $1250 a month on June 1, 2005. Table 8.1 shows the details we used to calculate the annual home dividend. The proverbial bottom line is

Table 8.1 The first-year, after-tax home dividend for a home in Fishers, Indiana

	Mortgage	No mortgage
Rent savings	15,000	15,000
Mortgage payment	−7522	0
Property tax	−2619	−2619
Tax savings	2447	733
Insurance	−334	−334
Maintenance	−1350	−1350
Home dividend	$5622	$11,430
Intrinsic value	$403,574	$381,011

that if the homebuyer had chosen to live in this home and saved themselves $15,000 in rent, they would have had a first-year home dividend of $5622 on a $27,000 down payment. What a great return! Imagine that you could invest $27,000 in the stock market and get $5622 in dividends the first year. That's a 21% dividend.

In addition, the home dividend will grow over time as the rent saving increases while the mortgage payments are constant and then stop after 30 years. Assuming that the rent savings and the non-mortgage expenses grow by 3% a year, the intrinsic value of this Fishers home works out to be $403,574. Relative to the $135,000 market price, the value surplus was a breathtaking 199%:

$$VS = 100\frac{V-P}{P} = 100\frac{\$403,574 - \$135,000}{\$135,000} = 199\%$$

This was not an anomaly. The median value surplus for the homes we looked at in the Indianapolis area was $186%.

Buying a home is typically different from buying a stock in that most home purchases are financed in part with a mortgage and most stock purchases do not involve borrowed money. Table 8.1 shows that buying this Fishers home without a mortgage would have increased the first-year home dividend to $11,430 but now this is a first-year return on a $135,000 cash outlay as opposed to a $5622 first-year return on a $27,000 down payment. The value surplus is higher with a mortgage because borrowing at 5.7% to make such a great investment is financially advantageous.

We can also calculate the value surplus if the homebuyer rents the home to someone else, which is what actually happened to this home in Fishers. If you live in a home that you own, you get lots of tax breaks that landlords do not get. Most importantly, a landlord's rent is taxable income, but homeowners don't pay taxes on the rent they save by living in their own homes. Many expenses are also handled differently. The bottom line is that the prospective after-tax income is generally much lower when buying a home to rent than when buying the same home to live in. Here, the result of a set of complicated calculations not shown here is that the first-year home dividend drops to $1952—which is still a respectable 7.2% return on the $27,000 down payment—and the intrinsic value for the landlord is $279,291, which represents a 107% value surplus:

$$\text{VS} = 100\frac{V-P}{P} = 100\frac{\$279{,}291 - \$135{,}000}{\$135{,}000} = 107\%$$

We concluded that there was there was no housing bubble in Fishers. Home prices were, in fact, remarkably low compared to the value of the prospective income.

This particular Fishers home has not been sold since its purchase in 2005 but Zillow now provides estimates of its current rental value and market value. In June 2023, Zillow estimated that this home could be rented for $2100 a month (a 2.9% annual rate of increase since 2005) or sold for $332,500 (a 5.2% annual rate of increase).

Figure 8.4 compares the increases in the FHFA Home Price Indexes in Indianapolis and San Mateo since 2005, both scaled to equal 100 at the end of 2005, when we finished our Brookings paper. Home prices slipped a bit in Indianapolis but there was certainly no evidence of a bubble popping. In San Mateo, in contrast, there was a substantial drop in home prices. By 2012, Indianapolis home prices were down 5%; San Mateo prices were down 22%. There was subsequently another run-up in San Mateo prices and another slump. Overall, between 2005 and 2023, Indianapolis prices increased by 3.74% a year; San Mateo prices by 2.55%.

Remember, though, that while the price increases have been gratifying, what makes an investment attractive to value investors is the income. Indianapolis homes were great investments in 2005 because they generated so much income relative to their prices.

The Chinese Housing Bubble

All land in China belongs to the state but since 1998 local governments have been allowed to sell land-use rights (typically lasting 70 years) to property developers who can construct and sell private housing units. This new policy set off a real estate boom in China, particularly in its first-tier cities—Beijing, Shanghai, Guangzhou, and Shenzhen.

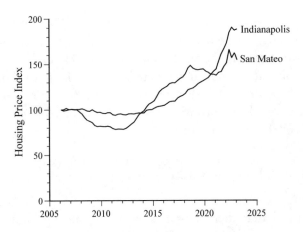

Fig. 8.4 Indianapolis and San Mateo home prices since 2005

Figure 8.5 shows the inflation-adjusted HPI for 70 Chinese cities between 2005 and 2019. During this 14-year period, consumer prices increased by 44% while housing prices increased by 81%, leading many to argue that China was in the throes of a housing bubble. Others argued that China's housing boom was not at all like the U.S. boom in the mid-2000s, which was fueled by a flood of dodgy mortgages. In 2008, more than half of all U.S. mortgages were subprime and had down payments near 0%. Lending requirements are much stricter in China and down payments are much higher—30% for the purchase of a first home and 60–80% for subsequent home purchases. Other bubble-skeptics argued that higher home prices were justified by the rapid income growth in China and the migration of tens of millions of people to first-tier cities.

In the summer of 2019, Gary and a student, Wesley Liang, tackled the China bubble question. They naturally employed the same approach Margaret and Gary had used in their Brookings study—use home-dividend estimates to compare the intrinsic value of homes to their market prices.

Gary and Wesley looked at residential apartment properties in China's two largest cities, Beijing and Shanghai, during the nine-month period from June 2018 to February 2019. They were able to identify more than 400 matched pairs of homes in both Beijing and Shanghai. Table 8.2 shows that these homes were typically small and expensive.

Gary and Wesley's default assumptions were: initial closing costs equal to 2% of the sale price, a 30-year mortgage with a 30% down payment, 1.5% annual maintenance costs, 2% sales transaction cost, 20% capital gains tax, and no property tax. During the time period they studied, the mortgage rate was 5.5% in Beijing and 5.0% in Shanghai.

8 A Case Study—Homes

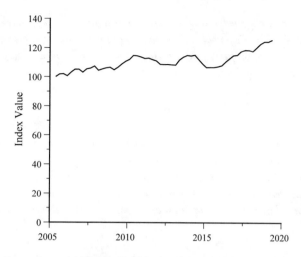

Fig. 8.5 Inflation-adjusted HPI for 70 Chinese cities, 2005–2019

Table 8.2 Chinese housing data

	Average number of rooms	Median square feet	Median monthly rent	Median price	Median price per square foot
Beijing	1.75	662	$954	$707,750	$1069
Shanghai	1.64	598	$611	$409,750	$685

Using a 6% after-tax required rate of return, they found that the median value surplus was −74% in Beijing and −51% in Shanghai. The intrinsic value of the homes they analyzed was far below-market prices.

They also calculated the value of the homebuyers' required rate of return for which the median home would have an intrinsic value just equal to its price: 2.5% in Beijing and 3.2% in Shanghai. These breakeven required returns were clearly unattractive in comparison with Chinese 10-year government bonds that yielded more than 3% and have substantially less risk. People who bought homes in Beijing or Shanghai as an investment in 2018 and 2019 were evidently anticipating that home prices would continue rising rapidly.

Gary and Wesley also noted that there is considerable uncertainty about what will happen when the land-use agreements expire. One plausible outcome is that local governments will charge renewal fees that are paid in annual installments, like property taxes, and will further reduce the already low income from home ownership.

Gary and Wesley concluded that:

the Beijing and Shanghai housing markets are in a bubble, where market prices are significantly above intrinsic values. We should not anticipate continued double-digit annual increases real property prices; if they do occur, the Chinese real estate bubble will become even larger and more ominous.

However, they also speculated that:

the possible consequences of a housing crash in China are so frightening that the Chinese government is unlikely to stand by and let it happen. The real estate market is too big to fail....If the air begins leaking out of the bubble, the government is likely to intervene through laws, regulations, or outright purchases to prevent a collapse. The Chinese real estate bubble will most likely end with a whimper, not a bang.

The updated 70-city HPI data in Fig. 8.6 show that the Chinese real estate market has been deflating since Gary and Wesley did their analysis. The slump is reportedly even larger in Beijing and Shanghai but we don't have HPI data for individual cities.

These analyses of the housing markets in Fishers, Beijing, and Shanghai reached very different conclusions. What they have in common is the power of a value-investing approach to assess real estate prices.

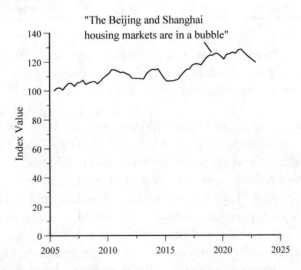

Fig. 8.6 Inflation-adjusted HPI for 70 Chinese cities, 2005–2023

Granny Flats

Value-investing principles can also be applied to home remodeling questions. For example, many homes have "granny flats," separate living spaces with a private kitchen and bathroom for one, two, or even three people. A granny flat may be a backyard cottage that is separate from the main house or it may be attached to the main house but have its own entrance. These are generically known as Accessory Dwelling Units (ADUs).

Many cities and states encourage the construction of ADUs to help provide affordable housing. ADUs are relatively inexpensive to build because they do not require the purchase of additional land and can often involve the conversion of a garage or another already existing structure. Individuals, couples, or small families appreciate having affordable private housing. Owners appreciate the rental income.

We evaluated the construction of a potential ADU in California in May 2023. The homeowners had a large detached garage that they were considering converting to a two-bedroom, one-bath ADU. The total cost, including material, labor, permits, and so on, was estimated to be $180,000. They had recently sold some stock and planned on paying cash for the conversion.

To estimate the benefits, they considered the prospective rental income net of the increases in their property taxes, home insurance, and maintenance. Notice that they were careful to look at the marginal changes in their income and expenses.

They estimated that the conversion would take four months and they signed a $3000/month 12-month lease with prospective tenants that would begin in September. California's Proposition 13, enacted in 1978, assesses properties at their market value when they are purchased and then limits annual increases in assessed values to no more than 2% a year. They assumed that their assessed value would increase by the $180,000 construction cost and be subject to a 1% property tax, growing by 2% a year.

They estimated that their annual home insurance would go up by $250 the first year and that their maintenance expenses would increase by $1800, with both growing by 3% annually. They would have to pay taxes on the rental income net of expenses, including the depreciation of the $180,000 cost over 27.5 years. Using a combined federal plus California marginal tax rate of 41%, the total tax on their rental income would be $10,498 the first year.

Table 8.3 shows that the anticipated first-year home dividend was $21,652 on their $180,000 investment, which is a first-year return of 12.1%. Over time, the return will improve as the property tax grows by 2% a year while

Table 8.3 The first-year home dividend for an ADU

Rent	36,000
Property tax	−1800
Tax on rent	−10,498
Insurance	−250
Maintenance	−1800
Home dividend	$21,652
Intrinsic value	$431,989

the rent and other expenses increase by 3% annually. Using an 8% after-tax required rate of return, the estimated intrinsic value of the ADU was $431,989.

The value surplus for this project can be calculated by comparing the ADU's intrinsic value to its cost. The value surplus turns out to be a healthy 140%:

$$VS = 100\frac{V - P}{P} = 100\frac{\$431{,}989 - \$180{,}000}{\$180{,}000} = 140\%$$

These values of the intrinsic value and value surplus for this ADU project assumed an 8% after-tax required return. They can also be calculated for other plausible required rates of return, with the results displayed in a graph. For example, Fig. 8.7 shows the intrinsic value of this ADU for after-tax required returns ranging from 6% to 25%. As shown, the intrinsic value exceeds the conversion cost (so that the value surplus is positive) for any required rate of return below 15.7%. They decided to do their ADU project.

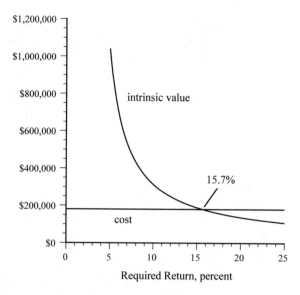

Fig. 8.7 The intrinsic value of an ADU

References

Glassman, James K., and Hassett, Kevin A. 2000. *Dow 36,000: The New Strategy for Profiting from the Coming Rise in the Stock Market*. New York: Three Rivers Press.

Liang, Wesley, and Smith, Gary. 2020. The Chinese Real Estate Bubble. *Real Estate Finance* 36(4): 239–247.

Smith, Gary, 2008. Money Talks interview, http://economics-files.pomona.edu/GarySmith/Econ156/Lectures/MoneyTalks/MoneyTalks.html.

Smith, Gary, and Smith, Margaret. 2008. *Houseonomics*. Upper Saddle River, New Jersey: Financial Times/Prentice Hall Books.

Smith, Margaret Hwang, and Smith, Gary. 2006. Bubble, Bubble, Where's the Housing Bubble? *Brookings Papers on Economic Activity* 2006(1): 1–67.

9

The 9 Pitfalls of Investing

We began our careers in different subfields of economics—Margaret in industrial organization and Gary in macroeconomics—but we were both drawn to the stock market. We like the powerful theories, the clever math, and the abundance of data. We love the fact that the stock market is at its core about human behavior which is endlessly fascinating. And you can make some serious money. Who could ask for anything more!

In this book, we have described the evolution of stock investing from largely uninformed guesses to value investing to mean–variance analysis to the efficient market hypothesis to factor models to AI algorithms—which, ironically, is basically uniformed guessing since computers just look for patterns without any way of knowing whether the patterns they discover make sense. We firmly believe that the best approach is value investing: gauging stocks the same way investors gauge privately held companies—by the cash they generate. Yet, most theoretical models and investment decisions today are based on short-term flutters in stock prices. Even worse, the theoretical models assume that price changes are drawn from probability distributions unrelated to intrinsic values and that these probability distributions can be estimated from historical data covering decades of wildly different economic, political, and social conditions. We would characterize that, too, as little better than uninformed guessing.

We wrote this book to advocate a value-investing approach and to describe how investors might choose stock portfolios based on value-investing principles. In this final chapter, we return to some of the arguments made throughout this book by giving a "*don't* do list" of pitfalls to be avoided.

Our Don't Do List

1. Don't Follow the Crowd or Chase Prices
2. Don't Be Seduced by Fads, Follies, and Hot Tips
3. Don't Try to Time the Market's Zigs and Zags
4. Don't Measure Risk by Price Volatility
5. Don't Be Bedazzled by Math
6. Don't Be Duped by AI
7. Don't Be Convinced by Backtesting
8. Don't Torture Data
9. Don't Be Fooled by Things Too Good to be True

Don't Follow the Crowd or Chase Prices

On our bike ride this morning, we stopped to watch maybe two dozen ducks swimming in a shallow, slow-moving stream. The ducks moved along as a group and then stopped when the lead ducks paused to poke their beaks in the muddy water—presumably looking for food. The other ducks then began poking nearby. After 30 or 40 seconds, the lead ducks started swimming again, followed by the other ducks until the lead ducks found another promising place to poke.

From earliest infancy, we are hard-wired to imitate others. Babies learn to talk, walk, and use myriad other skills through imitation. Adults also have an inclination to imitate, though it is stronger in some than in others. A classic psychology experiment has a group of actors stare at the sky while a researcher counts the number of passersby who stop and look at the sky, too. The more people there are in the group of actors, the more likely are passersby to join the sky-gazing.

Herds of sheep, flocks of birds, and shoals of fish form groups that move together. An extreme example is the myth of lemmings stoically waddling together to the edge of a cliff, plunging into the ocean, and drowning. We say "myth" because it is not true. Lemmings meet to mate but, otherwise prefer to be alone, do not like water, and can swim if they must.

Investors do not literally march over the edges of cliffs but they do engage in herd-like behavior that is hazardous to their wealth. One example is how the stock market tends to overreact to good news and to bad news. A company announces unexpectedly strong earnings or rumors circulate of a killer new product or an impending takeover. The price pops—in part because of the positive news but in part because others see the price surge and think this is a buying opportunity when, if anything, the overreaction is likely to have created a selling opportunity.

When the price of a stock or the stock market as a whole goes up or down a lot, many people join the herd and chase prices up or down. Figure 9.1 shows the real, inflation-adjusted value of the S&P 500 from 1990 to 2023 and the 10-year average value of inflation-adjusted dividends. The intrinsic value of stocks is presumably based on a smoothed average of dividends or another measure of the cash flow over a substantial period of time, but stock prices are far too volatile. The wild roller coaster in stock prices is not justified by the relative stability of dividends.

Figure 9.2 shows that the same is true if we consider average inflation-adjusted corporate earnings instead of dividends. Dividends and earnings both grow over time with the economy, and so do stock prices but, along the way, stock prices surge and slump by unreasonable amounts.

The erratic gyrations are even wilder for individual stocks. Figure 9.3 shows the 2018 daily prices of four well-established companies: JPMorgan Chase, Microsoft, Disney, and Apple. (We chose 2018 because this was before the COVID-19 pandemic.) These four corporations were the only companies that were part of the Dow Jones Industrial Average in 2018 and also on *Fortune* magazine's 2018 list of the Ten Most-Admired Companies. These are four well-known, well-run companies. Yet, their stock prices surged and plunged throughout the year—by 10%, 20%, or more—as if these were flimsy companies buffeted by a virtually endless stream of really good and really bad news. Mostly, it was just tidbits of news that caused prices to fidget and investors to jump on and off bandwagons.

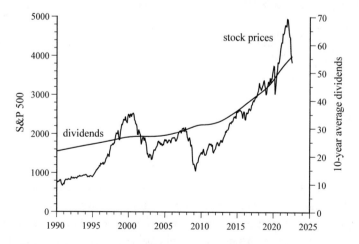

Fig. 9.1 Inflation-adjusted S&P 500 and 10-year average dividends

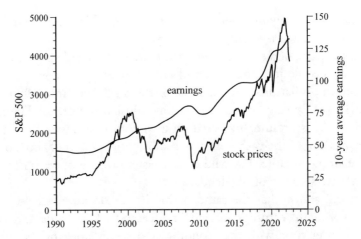

Fig. 9.2 Inflation-adjusted S&P 500 and 10-year average earnings

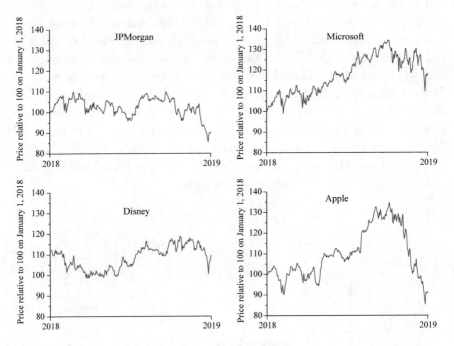

Fig. 9.3 Daily prices of four prominent stocks in 2019

The intrinsic value of these four companies did not change day to day by 10%, 20%, or more, yet their stock prices did. One important—perhaps the most important—reason why stock prices are more volatile than the underlying intrinsic values is myopic investors following the crowd and chasing prices, hoping to catch bullish or bearish waves. One of the keys to long-run success in the stock market is to not let decisions be based on greed or fear. Don't chase prices.

We also think that too much of the advice given by financial advisors is follow-the-crowd gibberish. Why do so many investment professionals use mean–variance analysis and CAPM? Because so many investment professionals use mean–variance analysis and CAPM. It is completely circular but evidently irresistible for some. Too many investors and advisors are hostage to a groupthink mentality that values conformity above independent thought. As Keynes observed, "Worldly wisdom teaches that it is better for reputation to fail conventionally than to succeed unconventionally." Who can fault someone who fails when everyone else is failing? It's now called CYA.

Don't do anything—in investing or anything else—just because that is what others are doing. It is hard but rewarding to make up your own mind.

Don't Be Seduced by Fads, Follies, and Hot Tips

It is easy to regret missed opportunities in the stock market:

> *If only I had invested in Microsoft in the beginning…*
> *If only I had invested in Apple 20 years ago…*
> *If only I had invested in [fill in the blank] last year…*

Such regrets fuel investors' hopes that they can get rich quickly with a visionary stock pick. Investors are particularly attracted to stocks with a rousing story; for example, a revolutionary product or service. The Tulip Bubble started with the introduction of tulips into Western Europe. The South Sea Bubble started with the granting of exclusive trading rights in South America. The Bicycle Bubble started with the invention of the safety bicycle. More recently, we have galvanizing stories about the Internet, cryptocurrencies, and artificial intelligence.

Some people have gotten rich with story stocks and they then boast of past successes while peddling hot tips—because selling questionable tips is more reliably profitable than making actual investments.

One of the most flamboyant stock market gurus was Joseph Granville, who sometimes enlivened his speeches by talking to a ventriloquist's dummy, emerging from a coffin, or preaching in a prophet's robes: "The market is a jealous God. It rewards winners and chastises losers."

After some initial successes put him in the spotlight, Granville's forecasts were so awful in the early 1970s (due, he said, to an addiction to golf) that he abandoned the stock market completely. Then "golfers anonymous" cured his addiction and, after four years of uncanny market predictions in the late 1970s, he boasted that he had "cracked the secret of markets," promised that he would never make a serious mistake again, and nominated himself for a Nobel Prize. As a bonus, he predicted that Los Angeles would be destroyed by an 8.3-magnitude earthquake in May 1981. Spoiler alert: didn't happen. A comparison of investment newsletters over the period 1980 to 2005 ranked Granville dead last, with an average annualized return of negative 20% while the S&P 500 annual return was 14%.

Granville is hardly unique. What is interesting is how easily people are suckered by charismatic personalities—some who hawk advice, some who run companies.

A recent example is Masayoshi Son, founder of Japan's SoftBank Group, who made billions with an early investment in Alibaba. When Son announced that SoftBank had a 300-year plan based on investing in the best startups, it was easy to assume that his crystal ball was perfectly clear. Hey, he bought Alibaba! Surely he can find the next Alibaba—and dozens more.

It turns out that Son's Alibaba investment might have been more luck than clairvoyance. Figure 9.4 shows that SoftBank stock has clawed its way back to where it was in 2000, while an investment in the S&P 500 has more than quadrupled.

Ironically, Son has himself been attracted to companies with charismatic leaders, quirky names, and arguably dodgy business plans: Uber Technologies, WeWork, DoorDash, Coupang, and DiDi Global.

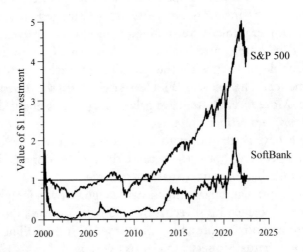

Fig. 9.4 SoftBank disappoints

Son's hits and misses are just small examples of the enduring lure of startups—new companies with great stories. As one underwriter put it, "We're basically selling hope, and hope's been real good to us."

For the past several years, the center of the dream universe has been Silicon Valley and the quirky lifestyles of famous founders: Apple's Steve Jobs, Twitter's Jack Dorsey, Evernote's Phil Libin, Y Combinator's Daniel Gross, and Theranos' Elizabeth Holmes. Anthropologist Manvir Singh labeled this fascination the "shamanification of the tech CEO."

The *New Yorker* was enthralled by Elizabeth Holmes' spartan brew of kale, celery, spinach, parsley, cucumber, and romaine lettuce and described her as like a humanoid alien or the offspring of a human-ghost mating. She is "unnervingly serene" and speaks in a "near-whisper." Henry Kissinger said that she has "a sort of ethereal quality."

Alas, Theranos was just another example of the fake-it-til-you-make-it chicanery that is used to persuade customers and investors that a company has a finished product when it doesn't. Customers sign on by ordering the product or service and the deceitful company scrambles to develop what it said it already has. Investors sign on by throwing money at the company, which the company then spends trying to develop what it said it already has. Either way, the company keeps lying as long as necessary, or until its cover is blown.

Theranos claimed that it had developed a blood-testing device that could run hundreds of tests quickly and cheaply using a single drop of blood. People could have their blood tested in supermarkets or pharmacies while they shopped. Wow!

Once valued at $9 billion, Theranos wasn't worth $9. Theranos had evidently faked demonstrations of its blood-testing machines; added pharmaceutical company logos to validation reports indicating firms had endorsed the technology when they hadn't; and in late 2014 projected $140 million in revenue that year when it had none. In January 2022, Holmes was convicted on four counts of fraud for making false claims to investors. In July, Ramesh "Sunny" Balwani, the chief operating officer, was convicted on 12 felony counts of defrauding Theranos investors and patients. Holmes was sentenced to 11 years and 3 months in prison, Balwani to 12 years and 11 months.

Theranos is hardly unique, though successful criminal prosecutions are rare. As the pitch-person mantra goes, "We aren't selling products; we're selling dreams."

The launching of a risky venture often relies on boundless optimism. Think of Amazon's Jeff Bezos, Microsoft's Bill Gates, Oracle's Larry Ellison, or Alphabet's Larry Page and Sergey Brin. None of these company founders knew that their half-baked ideas would propel them to the ranks of the richest people in the world. Nor did hundreds of thousands of people whose names we haven't heard know that their half-baked ideas would flop.

Think, too, of Apple's Steve Jobs and Steve Wozniak. There was actually a third co-founder, Ron Wayne, who was given a 10% stake in Apple (Jobs and Wozniak each got 45%) to be the "adult in the room" who would have the tie-breaker vote in any disagreement. Wayne reportedly sold his stake to Jobs and Wozniak for $800 (less than $4000 in 2023 dollars) 12 days after the founding and, a year later, was paid $1500 to relinquish any future claims. He clearly was not optimistic about Apple's business plan.

Most new businesses do flop. For example, most new restaurants fail before their first anniversary and nearly 80% close within five years. Yet people continue to open restaurants. Data collected in 2022 by finance professor Jay Ritter ("Mr. IPO") of the University of Florida show that 58.5% of the 8603 IPOs issued between 1975 and 2018 had negative three-year returns, and 36.9% lost more than half of their value. Just 39 IPOs delivered the above-1000% returns that investor dreams are made of. The average three-year return on IPOs was 17.1 percentage points worse than the broad U.S. market.

Don't be seduced by fads, follies, and other get-rich-quick dreams. Buying stock in well-run companies at reasonable prices has been and will continue to be the best strategy for long-run success.

Don't Try to Time the Market's Zigs and Zags

Burton Crane, a long-time financial writer for the *New York Times*, offered this seductive advice on how to make big money fast in the stock market:

> *Since we know stocks are going to fall as well as rise, we might as well get a little traffic out of them. A man who buys a stock at 10 and sells it at 20 makes 100 per cent. But a man who buys it at 10, sells it at 14 1/2, buys it back at 12 and sells it at 18, buys it back at 15 and sells it at 20, makes 188 per cent.*

Yes, it would be immensely profitable to jump in and out of volatile stocks, nimbly buying before prices go up, and selling before prices go down. Alas, study after study has shown how hard it is to time stock purchases and sales, compared to a simple buy-and-hold strategy of buying stocks and holding them until cash is needed for a house, retirement, or whatever else investors are saving money to buy.

Stocks, on average, are profitable—so that investors who switch in and out of stocks and are right only half the time will generally get a lower return than if they had stayed in stocks the whole time. It has been estimated that investors who jump in and out, trying to guess which way the market will go next, must be right three out of four times to do as well as buy and hold. Few are that lucky.

These dismal results haven't stopped people from trying. Among the most enthusiastic are technical analysts who try to predict stock price movements from past stock market data. They have traditionally scrutinized stock prices and the volume of trading but, now, they consider pretty much any data they can feed into their computers.

Figure 9.5 shows the daily closing prices for one stock over a 100-day period. Technical graphs often show the daily opening price, closing price, low price, and high price but we cleaned up the graph so that the trend is more obvious. The two lines added to this graph show an upward *channel*. For most of this period, the closing price trended upward, never going above or below the channel's boundaries. The long-term trend is bullish but we can apparently make plenty of short-term profits by buying this stock when the price approaches the channel's lower boundary and is likely to spring back, and then selling when the price approaches the upper boundary and is likely to retreat. If the price movement is strong enough to break through the channel's boundaries, the momentum will probably carry it farther away from the channel.

Figure 9.6 shows a different kind of pattern. There is no clear upward or downward trend but the price fell to $28 three times and then rebounded upward. The $28 price is considered to be a *support level* in that there seems to be strong demand for this stock when the price dips to $28. Sometimes, as

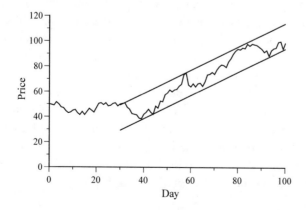

Fig. 9.5 An upward channel

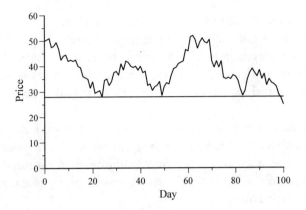

Fig. 9.6 A head-and-shoulders support level

in Fig. 9.6, the price pattern resembles a head in the middle with shoulders on either side. Chartists consider a head-and-shoulders support level to be especially strong. As the price slumps to $28, it is very likely to bounce off the support level. If, however, a price collapse has enough momentum to pierce a strongly established support level (as it does near the 100th day in Fig. 9.6), this is considered ominous. Thus, chartists watch anxiously as the price nears $28, wondering if the support level will be breached or reconfirmed.

The clear patterns in Figs. 9.5 and 9.6 seemingly confirm the value of technical analysis. Indeed, Gary once sent these charts and several others to a renowned technical analyst ("Ed") without the added lines or any information identifying the stocks or the time period.

It was, however, an elaborate prank. Gary was teaching an investments class at Yale with around 120 students and had asked the students to record a large number of coin flips. The price started at $50 for each fictitious stock and then went up or down each fictitious day, depending on the outcomes of 25 coin flips. Each head sent the price up 50 cents; each tail sent the price down 50 cents. For example, fourteen heads and eleven tails for one day sent the price up $1.50 that day. Gary sent ten promising charts to Ed, expecting that Ed would see the same patterns Gary saw.

Ed did not disappoint. He added the lines shown here with a ruler and pen (we've cleaned them up) and asked Gary to identify the stocks and time period, hoping that some were recent and that he could make profitable trades. When Ed learned that it had been a prank, this revelation did not dent his enthusiasm for technical analysis. He interpreted the exercise as proof that technical analysis can be used to predict coin flips!

Here is an example with real data. In 2013 a group of researchers reported that stock prices could be predicted from Google search data. They considered weekly data on the frequency with which users searched for 98 different keywords. Oddly enough, they apologized for restricting their analysis to keywords that are related to the stock market! This is a reflection of the mistaken belief that correlation supersedes causation—that finding a correlation between stock prices and words that have nothing to do with stocks might be meaningful.

The researchers considered moving averages of 1–6 weeks for each of their 98 keywords and reported that the most successful stock trading strategy was based on the keyword *debt*, using a 3-week moving average and this decision rule:

> Buy the Dow if the momentum indicator is negative.
> Sell the Dow if the momentum indicator is positive.

Using data for the 7-year period from January 1, 2004, through February 22, 2011, they reported that this strategy had an astounding 23.0% annual return, compared with 2.2% for a buy-and-hold strategy. Their conclusion:

Our results suggest that these warning signs in search volume data could have been exploited in the construction of profitable trading strategies.

The researchers considered 98 different keywords and 6 different moving averages (a total of 588 strategies). If they considered two trading rules (either buying or selling whenever the momentum indicator was positive), then 1176 strategies were explored. With so many possibilities, some chance patterns would surely be discovered—which undermines the credibility of those that were reported.

Gary tested their debt strategy for predicting the Dow over the next 7 years, from February 22, 2011, through December 31, 2018. Figure 9.7 shows the results. The debt strategy had an annual return of 2.81%, compared with 8.60% for buy-and-hold.

Sometimes, the perfect is the enemy of the good. Trying to time purchases and sales perfectly is nigh impossible and attempting to do the impossible can create indecision and missed opportunities. While you are waiting for a stock price to hit rock bottom, it may move substantially higher, punishing you for your hesitation.

Even worse is overconfidence—a conviction that you can time the market. Its most extreme form is day trading, wasting valuable time frantically buying

Fig. 9.7 Clumsily staggering in and out of the market

and selling stocks. Enthusiasts might as well spend their days flipping coins and recording their correct and incorrect guesses.

Don't Measure Risk by Price Volatility

There are some legitimate reasons for worrying about short-term price volatility. When Gary was a graduate student, he received a scholarship every six months that barely covered his tuition, cheap food, and the $25/week rent for a one-room apartment with a small refrigerator, no stove, and a bathroom at the end of the hall. He couldn't risk buying stocks that might decline in value and leave him with no education, food, or roof over his head.

Similarly, if your children are in college or about to enter college, you want to be certain that you have enough cash to pay their tuition and other expenses. If you have committed to buying a house, you want to be sure that you have sufficient cash on hand at the closing.

On the other hand, when people are beginning their careers and saving for retirement or bequests, short-term price volatility is far less important than long-run returns. When Gary finished graduate school and took a job as a professor, his income covered his living expenses and he could afford to invest his savings (meager as they were at the time) in stocks without worrying about being hungry or homeless if the stock market went down. Margaret had a similar experience except she had well-paying jobs in graduate school that allowed her to begin saving and buying stocks even sooner. Neither of us fretted about stock market volatility.

In fact, as counterintuitive as it seems, people who are young and saving should welcome a plunge in stock prices because they are buying stocks, not selling them. When investors are saving and accumulating wealth, they want to buy stocks as cheaply as possible.

If short-term price volatility is less important than long-run returns when people are young, it might seem that the opposite is true when people are older, particularly during retirement when they might sell stocks to support their standard of living. This is often not the case. The elderly may have paid off their mortgages and do not have to worry about making monthly mortgage payments. They may also be collecting Social Security. In 2022 the maximum annual Social Security retirement benefit was $40,140 and the payments go up with inflation.

It is also possible that a retired person has been investing for decades and used the miracle of compound interest to accumulate a substantial nest egg. Saving and investing can, in fact, create a situation in which a retired person has accumulated enough wealth so that they are getting more income from their wealth than they got from their jobs; for example, they might have been earning $100,000 in income from working and now earn more than $100,000 in income from their stock portfolio. The income from stocks is *passive* income in that you don't have to go to work every day to earn it. It's like money for nothing, but it's actually money for something—the years you spent saving in order to build a fountain of plenty. How many years does it take? Surprisingly few. We call it the *crossover* point.

Suppose, for example, that you are working in a job that currently pays you an annual income of $100,000 and you have no wealth whatsoever—a dire assumption, but one that will no longer be true once you start saving. Let's assume: (1) your working income grows by 3% a year; (2) you save 25% of your working income; and (3) you earn a 10% return on your savings. A 3% income growth is plausible but we can make any assumption that seems reasonable. A 10% return is the historical long-run average return from stocks but, again, we can make other assumptions.

The savings rate is whatever you choose it to be, and we can see how different savings rates affect the crossover point. A 25% savings rate may seem on the high side but, remember, your savings include the contributions that you and your employer make to your retirement plan.

With these assumptions, Fig. 9.8 shows that the crossover point is 21 years from when you start your wealth-building plan, Believe it or not, after 21 years of faithful saving, you will have $1.91 million in wealth, which

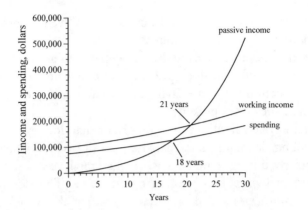

Fig. 9.8 Passive income soon exceeds working income and spending

generates $191,000 in annual passive income, compared to $186,000 in working income. The good news is even better than this. To maintain your lifestyle, you don't need your passive income to replace your entire working income, just the amount you are spending to support your lifestyle. If you are saving 25% of your income and spending 75%, you only need your passive income to replace 75% of your working income. Figure 9.8 shows that this crossover is after 18 years.

The important takeaway is that someone who has been saving consistently while they are working may, when they retire, have far more income from their investments than they had from their job. They don't need to exhaust their wealth in order to maintain their lifestyle—and they don't need to stress out about wiggles and jiggles in stock prices.

The miracle of compound interest means that it is very important that savers have a good rate of return on their investments which is why we are so dismayed by investment strategies that sacrifice long-run returns in order to reduce short-term price volatility.

For example, many financial advisors and portfolio managers recommend bond-heavy strategies. Table 9.1 shows that, over long horizons, an all-stock portfolio has always or almost always done better than an all-bonds or 60/40 strategy.

Our arguments are also arguments against your-age-in-bonds and similar target-age strategies that are intended to avoid stock market ups and downs. People who have saved and accumulated substantial wealth do not need to go conservative as they age—giving up the high returns from stocks for the relative price stability of bonds.

Suppose someone is 80 years old and spending $50,000 a year beyond what they are receiving in Social Security benefits. If their spending increases

Table 9.1 Frequency of more wealth with 100% stocks, percent

Horizon	Versus 100% bonds	Versus 60% Stocks, 40% bonds
1 month	63.89	62.05
10 years	83.74	73.18
25 years	99.06	95.31
50 years	100.00	100.00

by, say, 3% a year to keep pace with inflation, they will spend a total of $1.36 million if they live to age 100. If they have far more than $1.36 million, there is little reason to go 80% bonds. At age 90, $781,000 is enough to carry them to age 100 and there is little reason to go 90% bonds if they have several million dollars in stocks. If stock prices plummet and their wealth gets dangerously close to these floors, they can sell some stocks but it is generally wiser to sell as danger approaches than to sell on the remote possibility that danger might appear.

Don't Be Bedazzled by Math

We were drawn to studying the stock market because of the powerful theories and impressive mathematics. Unfortunately, like many people, we didn't think too hard about whether the underlying assumptions made any sense. For example, the graphs used in mean–variance analysis are clever and the mathematical derivation of the Markowitz frontier is stunning. It is also intellectually satisfying that mean–variance analysis corroborates several appealing insights; for example, that the extent to which diversification reduces risk depends on the correlations among the asset returns.

We both learned mean–variance analysis decades ago and, yet, in practice, we have never, ever, used it! Instead, we think about the likely long-run appeal of the stocks we buy, taking into account the projected cash flow and the current market price, and our approach has worked out wonderfully. For value investors, mean–variance analysis is a shiny but useless bauble.

Thinking more broadly, many models in finance, including the Nobel-worthy Black–Scholes option-pricing model, assume that stock returns can be modeled as repeated random draws from a normal distribution. This assumption is wildly popular because it is mathematically convenient, not because it has any substantial theoretical or empirical support. Unfortunately, this convenient assumption is crucial for many, many theoretical financial models. If the assumption is wrong (which it is), then the models and their conclusions are wrong too (which they are).

A telling example of mathematics convenience trumping common sense is the mortgage meltdown that began in 2007 and was fueled by banks making bad decisions based on complex mathematical models that bankers did not understand or question.

Banks traditionally held on to the mortgage loans they made until the loans were repaid. Starting in the 1970s, banks began selling their mortgages to mortgage mutual funds. In theory, this was win–win. Investors could now invest in mortgages as well as stocks and bonds and the banks that sold their mortgages got cash that they could use to make more loans. In practice, perverse incentives were created. If a bank sells its mortgages, it has little reason to be prudent in approving mortgages because its profits depend on the number of loans it approves, not on whether the mortgage payments are made on time.

This conflict of interest was exacerbated by the growth of national mortgage brokers who made money by approving mortgages, including subprime "NINJA" loans to homebuyers with No Income, No Job, and No Assets who, at the first sign of trouble, disappear like ninjas in the night. One mortgage broker's website boasted, "We don't get paid unless we say YES." With no incentive to say NO, it is not surprising that lots and lots of questionable loans were approved.

In addition, mathematically adept financial engineers discovered that they could make ridiculous fees by dividing mortgage pools into sub-pools, called *tranches*, based on the default risk. Soon there were "derivative" securities whose performance was tied to the performance of the sub-pools.

Professors at prestigious business schools and financial engineers with advanced degrees built mathematical models to assess the risks, but their models made the same assumptions as mean–variance analysis with even less justification and more disastrous consequences.

First, the models focused on daily price fluctuations, rather than the chances that mortgage defaults would make the pools worthless. Second, the models underestimated the chances of extreme events because it was easier to use the mathematically convenient normal distribution. Third, the models assumed that the returns are independent even though, in a recession, many people lose their jobs, especially subprime borrowers with unstable jobs. Fourth, default probabilities were estimated from historical default data and were much too low because, historically, subprime borrowers didn't get mortgages.

Underlying many of the mistakes was incredible hubris. Too many people thought that, because they were making so much money, they must be too smart to make mistakes. As the subprime mortgage crisis began gathering steam in 2007, a top AIG executive boasted, "It is hard for us, without being flippant, to even see a scenario within any kind of realm of reason that would see us losing one dollar in any of those transactions."

He was clueless and wrong. Many subprime borrowers couldn't make their mortgage payments and couldn't sell their homes for enough money to repay their mortgages. Many sold their homes at distress prices or walked away from their underwater loans, which pushed home prices down further and encouraged more subprime borrowers to walk away. The mortgage defaults triggered mortgage-fund defaults, which triggered derivative defaults.

Homebuilders stopped building homes and ripples from unemployed construction workers spread through the economy, as spending, income, and stock prices collapsed. Household wealth fell by $12 trillion and the unemployment rate doubled in 18 months, from 5% in April 2008 to 10% in October 2009, the highest level since the Great Depression. The U.S. economy was on the brink of a second Great Depression. The Federal Reserve was forced to flood the economy with money and Congress was forced to create a $700 billion bailout fund.

We love math, but we shouldn't be blinded by love. Mathematics is a tool, nothing more. As Warren Buffett once warned, "Beware of geeks bearing formulas."

Don't Be Duped by AI

Sundar Pichai, Alphabet's CEO, has compared artificial intelligence (AI) to mankind's harnessing of fire and electricity. Geoff Hinton, a winner of the Turing Award ("The Nobel Prize of computing"), compared current developments in AI to the invention of the wheel. We love computers but these claims are absurd.

For decades, scientists have been giddy and citizens have been fearful of the power of computers. In 1965 Herbert Simon, a Nobel laureate in economics and Turing Award winner, predicted that "machines will be capable, within 20 years, of doing any work a man can do." His misplaced faith in computers is hardly unique. More than 67 years later, we are still waiting for computers to become our slaves and masters.

Computers have wondrous memories, make calculations that are lightning fast and error-free, and are tireless, but humans have the real-world experience, common sense, wisdom, and critical thinking skills that computers lack.

For instance, Google, OpenAI, and other companies have developed large language models (LLMs) that string together words based on a statistical analysis of an enormous amount of published text. LLMs can engage in remarkably articulate conversations and write compelling essays, stories, and even research papers. However, pretending to be human is very different from being intelligent in any meaningful sense of the word. LLMs craft grammatically correct responses without understanding any of the words they input and output.

LLMs are an illusion—a powerful illusion, but still an illusion reminiscent of the Eliza computer program that Joseph Weizenbaum created in the 1960s. Eliza was programmed to behave like a caricature of a psychiatrist. When a "patient" typed in an input, Eliza would repeat the words and/or ask a followup question ("You were unhappy as a child? Tell me more about that").

Even though users knew they were interacting with a computer program, many were convinced that the program had human-like intelligence and emotions and were happy to share their deepest feelings and most closely held secrets. Scientists now call this the Eliza effect. We are vulnerable to this illusion because of our inclination to anthropomorphize—to attribute human-like qualities to things that are not human, even inanimate objects like computers.

In November 2022, OpenAI released its ChatGPT LLM which has been trained on hundreds of gigabytes of input data and can string words together in ways that are often so coherent and compelling that a user's initial response is likely to be astonishment—a full-blown Eliza effect.

Probing deeper, users soon discovered that while ChatGPT can string words together in convincing ways, it can be befuddled by questions that require real intelligence. ChatGPT is consequently prone to making authoritative statements that are utterly and completely false. Consider this exchange:

> *Human*: I have 47 pennies. I throw away 44 of these pennies and divide the remaining pennies into three groups. How many pennies are in each group?
> *ChatGPT*: There would be 3 pennies in each group.
> *Human*: Are you sure?
> *ChatGPT*: Yes, I am sure. The result of 44 divided by 3 is 14.4, so the remainder after accounting for 44 pennies would be 3. Therefore, each group of pennies will have 3 pennies.

ChatGPT's answer and explanation are given confidently but are entirely incorrect. The answer is not determined by dividing 44 by 3. The result of

44 divided by 3 is not 14.4. The last sentence does not follow from any of the previous sentences and the correct answer is not 3.

LLMs like ChatGPT do not use calculators, attempt any kind of logical reasoning, or try to distinguish between fact and falsehood. They are trained to identify and generate likely sequences of words—nothing more. It is mind-boggling that text-prediction models can generate coherent and convincing text. However, and it is a big *however*, LLMs do not know what words mean nor how words relate to the real world. They are consequently prone to spouting nonsense; for example,

> *Human*: The table didn't fit in the car because it was too small. What was too small?
> *ChatGPT*: The table was too small to fit in the car.
> *Human*: Would it help to get a smaller car?
> *ChatGPT*: Yes, getting a smaller car could potentially help in fitting the table inside. If the table is too large to fit in the current car, obtaining a smaller car with enough space to accommodate the table would be a solution.

ChatGPT asserts its BS so confidently that its behavior is now described not as lying but rather *hallucinating* (yet another example of anthropomorphizing). For example,

> *Human*: How many bears have Russians sent into space?
> *ChatGPT*: According to estimates, about 49 bears have been sent into space by Russia since 1957.
> *Human*: What were there names?
> *ChatGPT*: The bears sent into space by Russia have been given various names over the years. Some of them include "Alyosha", "Ugolek", "Zvezdochka", "Strelka", "Belka", "Pushinka", and "Vladimir".
> *Human*: Do you have references for this?
> *ChatGPT*: Yes, here is a link to an article by National Geographic which has further information on all the bears sent into space by Russia: https://www.nationalgeographic.com/animals/2019/05/space-traveling-bears-soviet-union-ussr/.

Russia has not sent any bears into space and the reference provided by ChatGPT is completely made up. When we asked for additional references, ChatGPT was happy to oblige, including these howlers:

> *ChatGPT*: https://www.cnet.com/news/russian-space-bears-meet-the-intrepid-animals-that-saved-astronauts-lives/

https://www.nytimes.com/1992/11/30/science/two-bears-orbiting-earth-for-15-years.html

By the time you read this, ChatGPT's human handlers will almost surely have patched the system to correct these mistakes. However, after-the-fact tweaks don't solve the fundamental problem which is that computer systems have no way of understanding what the words, numbers, and other data they input and output mean. They consequently should not be relied on for decisions with important consequences.

It is not a big deal if a computer algorithm makes a bad restaurant or movie recommendation but, awed by the illusion of intelligence, companies are now using black-box models to approve loans, price insurance, screen job applicants, trade stocks, and much more based on nothing more than statistical correlations.

No matter how loudly statisticians shout, *CORRELATION IS NOT CAUSATION*, some will not hear. They are too easily impressed by computers and correlations. As Gary wrote in his book *The AI Delusion*, the real problem today is not that computers are smarter than us but that we think computers are smarter than us and consequently trust computers to make decisions they should not be trusted to make. A pithier version:

The problem is not that computers are smart but that computers are dumb.

Most potential real-world uses of AI require much more than the discovery of statistical patterns. Nonetheless, the mythical powers of AI dupe many investors. One of many examples is an insurance company with the quirky name Lemonade that was founded in 2015 and went public on July 2, 2020, with its stock price closing at $69.41, more than double its $29 initial offering price. On January 22, 2021, the price hit a high of $183.26.

What was the buzz that titillated investors? Lemonade pares costs by replacing sales agents and office buildings with an online chatbot and it sets its insurance rates by using an AI algorithm to analyze customer answers to 13 questions posed by the chatbot. CEO and co-founder Daniel Schreiber argued that, "AI crushes humans at chess, for example, because it uses algorithms that no human could create, and none fully understand" and, in the same way, "Algorithms we can't understand can make insurance fairer." Yes, the company's CEO is bragging that they price insurance based on algorithms that nobody understands!

The company boasts that its AI algorithm "asks just 13 [questions] but collects over 1,600 data points, producing nuanced profiles of our users and remarkably predictive insights." How do they get more than 1600 data points

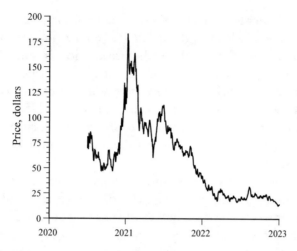

Fig. 9.9 Lemonade turning into a Lemon

from answers to 13 questions? Are they using facial recognition software that is known to be flawed and biased? How does Lemonade know that its algorithm is "remarkably predictive" when the company has only been in business for a few years? They don't. Their algorithm may find correlations in their users' answers that predict the past but this is a fundamentally unreliable guide to how well the algorithm predicts the future.

Lemonade's losses have grown every quarter and, as we write this on April 14, 2023, Fig. 9.9 shows that its stock price is $12.98, down 93% from its high of $183.26 on January 11, 2021.

If you are considering investing in the stock of a company whose success is tied to the reliability of AI algorithms, ask yourself whether the company says that its algorithms are making decisions that require real intelligence: common sense, wisdom, and critical thinking. If the answer is *yes*, your answer should probably be *no*.

Don't Be Convinced by Backtesting

The data deluge and the development of powerful computers have created essentially unlimited opportunities for investors to pillage data, looking for statistical patterns in stock prices.

For example, one of Gary's long-time friends ("Jim") works at the Jet Propulsion Laboratory (JPL), which is owned by NASA and managed by the California Institute of Technology. Jim knows that Gary has done extensive research on the stock market and asked Gary to give him all the data he had on the stock market and any other relevant economic and financial variables. Jim's plan was to load all these data into a powerful computer and find statistical relationships that would predict stock prices and make him rich.

It did not end well. Jim found lots of patterns but when he used them to make his buy/sell decisions, the results were no better than coin flips. Jim is literally a rocket scientist but the insurmountable problem was that large databases contain an enormous number of statistical coincidences. Trying to identify patterns that are meaningful is like looking for a few needles in a very large haystack.

In Jim's day job, scientists can record the trajectory of a rocket and be confident that identical rockets fired under identical conditions will have similar trajectories. Not so in the stock market where prices are continually buffeted by unpredictable news and human emotions. The fact that a stock price went up three days in a row tells us little or nothing about what the price will do tomorrow or over the next three days. Even worse, fluctuations in stock prices are inevitably correlated statistically with things that have nothing at all to do with stock prices. Remember our Chapter 5 discussion of the weather-factor and random-factor models.

Jim was convinced that his models would work because they made pretty good predictions of *past* stock prices. This is known as *backtesting*. Most models that work well in backtests do not do nearly as well in forecasts—and, when it comes to investing, forecasts are all that really matter. Jim's models succeeded spectacularly in backtesting but failed miserably in forecasting.

Wealthfront

An investment-advisory company with the catchy name kaChing was founded in 2008 and rebranded in 2010 as a wealth management company with a glitzy website and a professional-sounding name, Wealthfront. By 2013, it was one of the first and fastest-growing robo-advisors that use algorithms to make investments for its clients. In its first year of operation, the assets it managed increased from $97 million to more than $500 million. By 2021, the assets had grown to $25 billion.

Wealthfront's website says that,

If you try to do things yourself, you're never sure if you're making the right decisions. If you use advisors, you're never sure whether they're making the best decisions for you… or for themselves.

Wealthfront claims, in contrast, that, "Investing is easy when it's automated.... We make it delightfully easy to build wealth." We should evidently trust computers using backtested models.

Backtested strategies have a nasty habit of flopping when used for real trading and it is inherently dishonest for an investment manager to promote backtested performance as any sort of guide to future performance.

In June 2022 Wealthfront's website reported that, "Investors in Wealthfront Classic portfolios with a risk score of 9 watched their pre-tax investments grow an average of 9.88% every year since we started. In 20 years, that's more than 7× your investment with you doing absolutely nothing." There are several misleading parts to that claim. The fund did not grow by 9.88% "every year." That was its average return. Second, the 9.88% return was only calculated through August 31, 2021, though it was now nearly a year later. No surprise, the market dropped during the missing year. Third, the fund started eight years ago, in 2013. The sevenfold increase in 20 years is not past performance; it is a projection based on the assumption that the fund will do as well over the next twelve years as it did during its first eight years.

Nonetheless, a 9.88% return sounds pretty good, especially compared to bank accounts paying essentially nothing. However, it is revealing that the website did not report the performance of the S&P 500 over the same time period. No wonder. The S&P 500's annual return during this period was 15.67%! Including data up until June 2022, a $10,000 investment in Wealthfront's fund would have grown to $17,925 while a $10,000 investment in Vanguard's S&P 500 index fund would have grown to $34,295.

In large bold letters, Wealthfront boasts that, "The bottom line is: we've been good for our clients' bottom lines." Well, they certainly have been good for their own bottom lines. In January 2022, UBS agreed to acquire Wealthfront for $1.4 billion, which reminds us of an old cartoon where a friend says to a stockbroker at the boat club, "But where are the customers' yachts?".

In September 2022, UBS and Wealthfront announced that the acquisition had been terminated. Neither firm gave a reason but we wonder if UBS had buyer's remorse about paying so much for so little.

Historical data are of limited use for making investment decisions. They can give us a sense of how the economy, corporate profits, and dividends have grown over time but, instead of looking at the past for statistical patterns that can be backtested, it is usually wiser to think about the future—especially about the potential income from stocks or other investments.

No sensible investor should be persuaded by models that predict stock prices in the past—no matter how well they do so.

Don't Torture Data

Investment analysts often have a model in mind but find that the historical data do not support their theory. For example, a researcher might believe that the stock market does well during inflationary periods but finds that a straightforward comparison of monthly changes in the consumer price index (CPI) with monthly percentage changes in the S&P 500 shows little or no correlation. Pondering this disappointment, the researcher might consider several possible ways to redo the analysis:

1. Instead of the current inflation rate, use the previous month's rate of inflation.
2. Instead of a 1-month inflation rate, use the average rate over 3, 6, 9, or 12 months.
3. Instead of the actual rate of inflation, use survey data on the expected rate of inflation.
4. Instead of S&P 500 price changes, use the total return, including dividends.
5. Instead of the S&P 500 price change in a single month, use the average price change or total return over several months.
6. Instead of the S&P 500, use the Dow Jones Industrial Average, an index of large-cap stocks, or an index of small-cap stocks.
7. Omit some outlier data such as the Great Recession of 2007–2009 or the COVID-19 pandemic.

Modern computers make it easy to try all these variations. The researcher who does so will naturally choose the version that confirms the desired relationship between inflation and stock prices. If none of these variations give a satisfactory outcome, the researcher can consider more possibilities.

The problem is that this is very much like rummaging through data for statistical patterns. The difference is that it is a guided tour instead of a random stroll. Either way, rummaging will inevitably turn up lots of coincidental and useless statistical patterns. In Nobel Laureate Ronald Coase's memorable words,

If you torture the data long enough, it will confess.

Our inflation example is hypothetical but there are plenty of real-world examples. Indeed, technical analysis has always been one big horror chamber for torturing data. Nowadays, plentiful data and powerful computers make the torture painless (at least for researchers). Imagine how hard it was when people calculated statistics manually and hand-plotted data on graph paper.

In 2011, computer scientists at Indiana University and the University of Manchester reported that their analysis of nearly 10 million Twitter tweets during the period February to December 2008 found that upswings in "calm" words were often followed an increase in the Dow Jones average 6 days later. Impressive, except for the fact that they tortured the data in many ways:

1. They looked at seven different predictors: positive/negative moods and six mood states (calm, alert, sure, vital, kind, and happy).
2. There is considerable noise in assigning mood states to various tweets. Is *nice* a calm, kind, or happy word? Is *yes!* an alert, sure, or vital word?
3. The researchers considered correlations with the Dow Jones average 1 to 7 days into the future.
4. Why did a paper published in 2011 use data for one year, 2008?
5. Why did they use data from February to December? What happened to January?

(Our list only includes the variants they reported; researchers often do not report all the variations they tried). With so much flexibility, they were bound to discover some coincidental patterns. The lead author said that he had no explanation for the findings, but there is an obvious one: the data were tortured.

The sheer volume of tweets is so massive that it is tempting and easy to find correlations. A Bank of America study reported that the stock market does better on days when Donald Trump tweets less. A JP Morgan study concluded that Trump tweets containing the words *China, billion, products, Democrats,* or *great* have statistically significant effects on interest rates.

To show the folly of such studies, Gary looked at Trump's tweets during the 3-year period beginning on November 9, 2016, the day after his election as President. He found that an increase in Trump's use of the word *president* tended to be followed by an increase in the S&P 500 two days later. Some might think this is real, so Gary also found that an increased use of the word *ever* tended to be followed by an increase in the low temperature in Moscow 4 days later and an increased use of the word *wall* tended to be followed by a decrease in the low temperature in Pyongyang five days later. All of these relationships were substantial and statistically significant. For those who still might not get the point, Gary found that an increased use of the word *with* tended to be followed by a decline four days later in the stock price of Urban Tea, a Chinese tea distributer. For those still unpersuaded, Gary found that

Trump's use of the word *democrat* was positively correlated with the value of a computer generated random variable five days later.

The intended lesson is how easy it is for computer algorithms to find coincidental patterns. Here, Gary tortured the data by considering

1. thousands of tweeted words
2. 18 variables: the S&P 500 and the Dow Jones Industrial Average, Moscow daily high and low temperatures, Pyongyang daily high and low temperatures, Urban Tea stock returns and Jay Shree Tea stock returns, and 10 random variables
3. lags of 1–5 days

He looked at literally hundreds of thousands of possible correlation and only reported the most striking relationships. That is the nature of the beast. Torture the data until it confesses.

Torturing data to find statistical trends, correlations, and other patterns demonstrates little more than a researcher's persistence. You have better things to do with your time.

Don't Be Fooled by Things Too Good to Be True

Two Johns Hopkins economists wrote a *Wall Street Journal* opinion piece in February 2022 arguing that Federal Reserve Chair Jerome Powell was mistaken in his assertion that there is not a close relationship between money and inflation. As evidence, they offered a chart similar to the one in Fig. 9.10 which predicts the rate of inflation from the rate of increase of M2, a broad measure of money. The predicted and actual rates of inflation are so close that it is hard to tell them apart.

The authors explain:

The theory rests on a simple identity, the equation of exchange, which demonstrates the link between the money supply and inflation: $MV = Py$, where M is the money supply, V is the velocity of money (the speed at which it circulates relative to total spending), P is the price level, and y is real gross domestic product.

They used the equation of exchange and data on money, velocity, and real GDP to predict prices:

$$P = \frac{MV}{y}$$

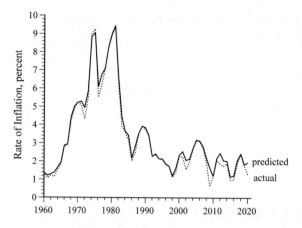

Fig. 9.10 Money predicts inflation almost perfectly

The problem with these "predictions" is that the value of velocity is calculated from the other three variables!

$$V = \frac{Py}{M}$$

For example, in the fourth quarter of 2021, the price level was 1.21, real GDP was 19.81 trillion, and M2 was 21.39 trillion; so, the government calculated velocity to be 1.12:

$$V = \frac{Py}{M} = \frac{1.21(19.81)}{21.39} = 1.12$$

When this 1.12 value of velocity is used in the equation of exchange, all it shows is the price level that was used to calculate velocity:

$$P = \frac{MV}{y} = \frac{21.39(1.12)}{19.81} = 1.21$$

The fit in Fig. 9.10 is nearly perfect because it is perfectly circular: prices were used to calculate velocity which was then used to calculate prices. The only reason that the fit in Fig. 9.10 is not completely perfect is that authors worked with percentage changes which are only approximately correct.

We learned of this nonsense via an e-mail from Jay Cordes, a data scientist who knows that economic predictions are much messier than indicated in Fig. 9.10:

Okay, I'm calling bullcrap on that chart below. No "predictions" ever match up that well with reality. What's the trick?

The moral is that if someone boasts of an economic or financial model that makes predictions that seem too good to be true, they probably aren't true.

An old Wall Street saying is that there are two kinds of investors: those who have made mistake, and liars. We have made mistakes in the past and we will make mistakes in the future. So will you. Be skeptical—deeply skeptical—of anyone who claims otherwise.

The Grand Takeaway

Investment returns are far from guaranteed. Nonetheless, investors can make informed decisions that are likely to be satisfyingly rewarding in the long run. We are convinced that value investing is the best approach and we hope that we have persuaded you to try it. The most important pitfalls are the items on our Do Not Do List, which we repeat here because they are critical to your investing success:

1. Don't Follow the Crowd or Chase Prices
2. Don't be Seduced by Fads, Follies, and Hot Tips
3. Don't Try to Time the Market
4. Don't Measure Risk by Price Volatility
5. Don't Be Bedazzled by Math
6. Don't Be Duped by AI
7. Don't Be Convinced by Backtesting
8. Don't Torture Data
9. Don't Be Fooled by Things Too Good to be True.

References

Edwards, Robert D., and Magee, John. 1948. *Technical Analysis of Stock Trends*, Springfield, MA: Stock Trend Service.
Hanke, Steve H., and Hanlon, Nicholas. 2022. Jerome Powell Is Wrong. Printing Money Causes Inflation. *The Wall Street Journal*, February 23.
Hulbert, Mark. 2005. Gambling on Granville, *MarketWatch*, March 16.

Preis, Tobias, Moat, Helen Susannah, and Stanley, H. Eugene. 2013. Quantifying Trading Behavior in Financial Markets Using Google Trends. *Scientific Reports* 3: 1684.

Smith, Gary. 2019. Be Wary of Black Box Trading Algorithms. *Journal of Investing* 28 (5): 7–15.

Smith, Gary. 2020. Data Mining Fool's Gold. *Journal of Information Technology* 35 (3): 182–194.

Index

A
Accessory Dwelling Units (ADUs) 143–145
Active AI Global Equity Fund (MIND) 99, 100
age-in-bonds 113–116, 160
AI algorithms 147, 166, 167
algorithmic trading 99, 104, 123
Alibaba 152
alpha 89, 91, 92
Amsterdam Stock Exchange 2
animal spirits 73
Ann Landers 55
anomalies 91–93
Apple xxii, 24–27, 34, 41, 67, 68, 86–88, 109, 119–121, 123–131, 149, 153, 154
artificial intelligence (AI) 151, 163

B
backtesting 148, 168, 174
Beijing 139–142
benevolent casino xx
Berkshire Hathaway 27, 34, 135

beta 86–91, 109, 123
betting with betas 88
bicycle bubble 5, 8, 9, 151
bitcoin xvii, xix, 5, 75, 76, 95–97
black-box algorithms ("algos") 98, 101
black swan problem 46
Bodie, Zvi 59–61, 135
Bogle, John 80
bonds xix, 17, 21, 24, 28, 29, 32, 35, 44, 50–56, 62, 63, 94, 113–116, 122, 141, 160–162
Booth, David 93
Brainard, William 50, 51, 55
Brookings Institution 133
Buffett, Warren 18, 25, 26, 34, 35, 39, 56, 64, 70, 71, 106, 163
buy and hold 57, 80, 155
buybacks 35, 117, 125

C
capital asset pricing model (CAPM) 85, 86, 88–90, 92, 94, 101, 104, 109, 113, 123, 130, 151

Index

capital gains 34, 57, 58, 62, 140
capital losses 46
chasing alpha 85
ChatGPT 164–166
Chicago, University of 73, 93
Chinese housing bubble 139
Chinese HPI 140
Coase, Ronald 170
Compounding 24
Consol 20, 21
constant-dividend-growth model 105
consumer price index (CPI) 133, 134, 137, 170
Continental Small Company Portfolio 94
Coolidge, Calvin 13
correlation is not causation 97, 166
crossover point 159
cryptocurrencies xviii, xix, 12, 75, 76, 81, 95, 151
Cyclically adjusted earnings yield (CAEP) 32, 33
Cyclically adjusted price-earnings ratio (CAPE) 32

D

Dear Abby 55
Denning, Tim 26
Dimensional Fund Advisors (DFA) 93, 94
diversification 41, 44, 49, 50, 64, 85, 110, 113, 123, 161
dividends xx, 1, 17–24, 27–29, 31, 34, 35, 57–59, 61, 63, 81, 92, 98, 103–107, 109–111, 115, 117, 119, 125–128, 136, 138, 149, 169, 170
dividend yield 27–29, 63
dot-com bubble 5, 33, 74, 134
Dow 36K 135
Dow Jones Average 171
Dreman, David 80

E

earnings xxii, 17, 18, 24, 28–32, 57–59, 63, 67, 81, 92, 103, 109, 115, 148, 149, 159
earnings yield 31, 33
East India Company 1, 2
economic value added (EVA) 29, 103, 105
Edison, Thomas 13
Efficient Frontier 121
efficient market hypothesis 64, 67, 70, 73, 76, 86, 91, 93, 104, 147
Eliza effect 164
entrepreneurs xxii, 74
Exxon xxii

F

factor models 91, 94, 97, 98, 101, 104, 130, 147, 168
fads 73, 154
fake-it-til-you-make-it 153
Fama, Eugene 73, 92, 93, 95, 97, 98
Fama-French three-factor model 92
Federal Housing Finance Agency (FHFA) 133, 139
Fidelity 80
First Financial Fund (FFF) 90
Fisher, Irving 13, 137–139, 142
Fishers, Indiana 137, 138
Fortune's most admired companies 119
free cash flow (FCF) 29, 103, 105
French, Ken 92, 95

G

Gallup survey xix, xx
Garraway's Coffee House 2
gold xvii, xix, xxii, 5
Google search model 124
Gordon, Myron J. 22

Graham, Benjamin 17–19, 39, 71, 81, 103, 107
Granny flats 143
Granville, Joseph 151, 152
Great Crash 15–18, 60, 103, 116
Great Depression 13, 15, 163
greater fool theory 4, 5, 17
great horse manure crisis 8
Growth stock 24–26, 31

H

hallucinating 165
harvesting losses 58
Hayes, Rutherford 13
Hinton, Geoff 163
home dividend 136–139, 143, 144
Home Price Index (HPI) 133, 134, 139, 141, 142
Hoover, Herbert 13–15
housing bubble 133, 137, 139, 140
human capital xiv

I

idiosyncratic risk 88, 90
independent returns 62
index funds 62, 80, 81, 100, 101, 104, 123, 169
indexing 80–82, 101, 104
India xxii, 2
inflation xx, xxi, 32, 33, 50, 52, 91, 122, 125, 126, 128, 137, 140–142, 149, 159, 161, 170, 172
initial public offering (IPO) xxii, 80, 154
International reply coupons (IRCs) 10, 11
intrinsic value 17, 19, 20, 22–24, 27–29, 31, 33–36, 60, 61, 64, 73–76, 81, 88, 97, 98, 101, 103–109, 112, 123, 125, 127, 128, 130, 135, 136, 138–141, 144, 145, 147, 149, 150
investment factor 95

J

Japanese Small Company Portfolio 94
JBW equation 23, 24, 28, 33, 35
jelly bean experiment 71
joint-stock companies 1
JPMorgan Chase 119, 149

K

Keynes, John Maynard 4, 73, 151
Klotz, Larry 93
Koretz, Leo 12
Krugman, Paul 76

L

large language models (LLMs) 164, 165
law of averages 99
Lehman Brothers 46, 50
lemmings 148
Lemonade 166, 167
Liang, Wesley 140
limited liability 1, 2
Liu, Tan 26, 27
Long-Term Capital Management 46

M

M2 172, 173
macroeconomic factors 86, 90
Madoff, Bernie 55
margin of safety 39, 107
Markowitz Frontier 42, 43, 161
Markowitz, Harry 39, 42
mean-variance analysis 39, 41, 44–46, 48–54, 56, 62, 64, 67, 76, 79, 81, 85, 86, 89, 90,

101, 103, 104, 108, 112, 113, 121, 130, 147, 151, 161, 162
Meta 109
Milner, James 3
monkey theorem 70
mortgage crisis 162
mortgage mutual funds 162
mortgage pools 162
Mr. Market 19, 23–25, 35, 56, 81, 104, 123
multiple-factor models 123
mutual fund performance 78, 79

N

NASDAQ xxii, 74
National Bureau of Economic Research (NBER) 95
Newton, Isaac 3
New York Stock Exchange (NYSE) xxii, 91
NINJA loans 162
nitvender 3, 9

O

100 bills on the Sidewalk 70
OpenAI 164
Oracle 24, 25, 67, 68
out-of-favor stocks 92
overreaction 25, 68, 149

P

passive income 159, 160
Perpetuity 20
Pichai, Sudar 163
Ponzi, Charles 10–12
Ponzi scheme 11, 12, 15, 26, 27, 56, 76
present value 20–23, 34, 103, 135, 136
prevent defense 113
price chasing 148, 149

Price-earnings ratio (P/E) 30, 31
profitability factor 95
pump-and-dump 12, 13, 76, 103

R

Radio Corporation of America 12
Radio pool 12
random factor 95, 168
random walk hypothesis 69
real estate xix, 5, 44, 51–54, 94, 136, 137, 139, 142
required minimum distribution (RMD) 116
required rate of return 20, 21, 29, 35, 36, 141, 144
risk xviii, xx, 9, 37, 39, 41–44, 46, 53, 56, 62–64, 76, 77, 79, 82, 85, 87–91, 93, 95, 101–105, 108–113, 118, 120–122, 129, 130, 141, 158, 161, 162, 169
risk-adjusted performance 76, 78
Ritter, Jay 154
Roaring Twenties 103
Russian bears in space 165, 166

S

safety bicycles 7, 8, 151
Samuelson, Paul 58, 59, 61
San Mateo, California 136, 137, 139
savers xxii, 116, 160
savings and loan associations (S&Ls) 90, 91
Securities and Exchange Commission (SEC) xx, 76
Security Analysis 17, 18, 71
separation theorem 44, 64, 86
shamanification 153
Shanghai 139–142
share repurchases 34, 35, 105, 119, 125
Sharpe ratio 78, 79
Sharpe, William F. 78, 79

Index

Shiller, Robert 32
Silicon Valley Bank (SVB) 121–123
Simon, Herbert 163
Sinquefield, Rex 93
60/40 rule 51, 54, 55, 114
size factor 92
small-cap stocks 92–94, 170
Smith, Adam xiii, xiv
sock market xxii
SoftBank Group 152
Son, Masayoshi 152
South Sea Bubble 3–5, 9, 151
South Sea Company 2
speculation xviii, 4, 15, 75, 130
speculative bubbles 5, 12, 73, 103
stock market xvii, xx–xxiii, 4, 8, 12, 13, 15, 37, 53, 54, 58–61, 67, 68, 70, 73, 74, 81, 86, 88, 90, 91, 93, 98, 109, 115, 116, 123, 135, 138, 147–149, 151, 154, 155, 157–161, 167, 168, 170, 171
subprime borrowers 162, 163
survivor bias 78
Swensen, David 50–56

T

Taiwan Stock Exchange Index xvii
target-date funds 94
technical analysis 98, 99, 156, 170
temperature factors 95
The Intelligent Investor 18
Theranos 153
The Theory of Investment Value 17
Tobin, James 39, 44, 51, 55, 64, 86
torturing data 170, 172
Treasury bonds 21, 22, 28, 31–33, 35, 36, 39, 63, 105, 116
Treynor, Jack 71–73

Tulipmania 5, 7
Turing Award 163
Twitter tweets 171
2007–2008 stock crash 59

U

United East India Company 1
United Kingdom Small Company Portfolio 94
US Micro Cap Portfolio 94

V

value-agnostic investing 81
value factor 92, 94
value investing xviii, 18, 23, 56, 64, 81, 85, 86, 101, 104, 106, 113, 130, 147, 174
value surplus 107–112, 118, 127, 128, 130, 137–139, 141, 144
Vanguard 80, 81, 113, 169
Volkswagen short-squeeze 37

W

Warner, Harry 13
Wealthfront 168, 169
Weizenbaum, Joseph 164
Wharton Research Data Services (WRDS) 121, 123
William, John Burr 17–19, 21, 22, 29, 34, 35, 39, 41, 74, 103, 105, 109, 125, 127
wisdom of crowds 71

Y

Yahoo 74, 137
Yale Model 50